MASTERING THE IPHONE SE 2020

THE COMPLETE USER GUIDE AND MANUAL FOR NEWBIES GETTING STARTED WITH THE SECOND GENERATION SE IPHONE

JAMES NINO

You are welcome to join the <u>Fan's Corner, here</u>

Mastering the iPhone SE 2020

The Complete User Guide and Manual for Newbies Getting Started with the Second Generation SE iPhone

James Nino

Disclaimer

The advice and strategies found within may not be suitable for every situation. This work is sold with the understanding that neither the author nor the publisher is held responsible for the results accrued from the advice in this book.

Contents to Expect

Chapter One

Overview of the iPhone SE 2020

In April 2020, Apple released a new smartphone - the iPhone SE 2020 (SE for Special Edition). Based on the reviews so far, it is being referred to as the idea substitution for the iPhone 8, and the replacement of the first iPhone SE.

Unboxing The iPhone SE 2020

On cutting open the sealed box, you should find the iPhone SE 2020 itself, an iPhone logo sticker pad, the manuals, Apple USB Lightning Cable, a 5W USB power adapter connector, lighting connector EarPods, and the Sim ejector pin.

Design

The iPhone SE 2020 is a near-perfect smartphone with a similar tough glass and aluminum structure of the iPhone 8. It comes in three color alternatives for users to choose from, they include; black, white, and red.

The iPhone SE body dimensions are an estimated 5.45 in height x 2.65 in width x 0.29 in depth (inches) and 5.22 ounces. The iPhone SE 2020's structure additionally has IP67 rating against water, which implies it may be submerged in 1 meter of water for as long as 30 minutes.

On the front side of the phone, the first noticeable feature is the 4.7-inch screen embedded with a retina HD display with IPS technology, an all-round strengthened glass screen with Haptic Touch. The front side also has huge black bezels above and below the screen. At the top of the screen, there's a seven-megapixel front camera (7 MP) and a microphone. At the lower bezel, there's a Touch ID home button for fingerprint-based biometric authentication.

At the rear side, there's a single-lens 12-megapixel camera with an f/1.8 aperture, a rear microphone, and a Light Emitting Diode with true tone flash. On the side of the phone are the volume buttons, the power button, and the SIM tray port.

Coming to the bottom part of the iPhone SE 2020, you will find the speakers and the lighting port.

Included Accessories

EarPods with Lightning Connector

Used to listen to music, watch recordings, videos, and make calls. The iPhone SE 2020 doesn't have an earphone jack, so EarPods with a 3.5 mm Headphone Plug won't be compatible with this model.

Apple USB Lightning Cable

Used to connect the iPhone to a PC and also to the USB charger adapter for charging.

SIM Eject Tool

Used to eject the iPhone's SIM tray.

Software

The iPhone SE is equipped with the latest A13 Bionic chip which is also present in the other 13th generation iPhones. Apple has called it its fastest chip ever in a cell phone.

Additionally, it gives the iPhone more power-efficiency, which improves battery life.

The Neural Engine controls the camera framework and increased reality applications. There's also a Machine Learning Controller that adjusts execution and productivity. As indicated by Apple, the A13 Bionic matched with iOS 13 empowers new applications that utilize AI and Core ML.

The iPhone SE 2020 is embedded with a 3GB RAM and is available in 64, 128, and 256GB storage options.

Installing A Sim Card into the Phone

Before setting up the iPhone SE 2020, it is important to note that you will require a Nano-SIM and/or eSim card is required to utilize cellular services when associating with GSM systems, some CDMA, or LTE networks. An iPhone actuated on a CDMA remote system can likewise utilize a Nano-SIM card for interfacing with a GSM system, principally for universal roaming. Your iPhone is bound to your remote specialist co-op's policies.

Removing the SIM Card Tray

Insert a paper clip or the SIM discharge instrument into the little opening of the SIM card plate on the right side of the iPhone SE 2020. At that point, press to discharge the plate. Station the SIM card in the plate—the calculated corner decides the right direction—then embed the SIM card plate again into the iPhone SE 2020.

Setting a SIM Pin

To shield your SIM card from others utilizing it for calls or cellular data, you can utilize a SIM PIN. With a SIM PIN, each time you restart your iPhone SE 2020 or expel the SIM card, your SIM card locks, and you see "LOCKED SIM" in the status bar.

To set it up, go to Settings, then continue to the Phone option.

Switching the iPhone SE 2020 on and off

Press and hold the power button until the Apple logo shows up.

Switching off the iPhone SE 2020

Hold the power button down until the slider shows up, then drag the slider to the switch-off side.

The iPhone can be set up over a Wi-Fi network, or over your carrier's cellular network (not accessible in all zones). You can likewise set up the iPhone by associating it to a PC and utilizing iTunes.

Getting ready for setup

To make the setup as smooth as possible, you must have the following things within your reach:

1. The name and passkey (if appropriate) of your Wi-Fi networks.

Your Apple ID and password; if you don't have an Apple ID, you can sign up for one during the setup.

2. Your credit or debit card account information if you need to add a card to Apple Pay during setup on supported variants.

3. Your previous iPhone's backup data if you're changing to the iPhone SE 2020 from another iPhone. Your Android gadget, if you want to move from Android to iOS.

Chapter Two

Set up iPhone

Turn on your iPhone, then follow the setup aide. If you have another iPhone, iPad, or iPod touch with iOS 11, you can securely duplicate a significant number of your settings, preferences, and iCloud Keychain to your new iPhone SE 2020. Hold your other device near your new iPhone SE 2020, and wait for the automatic setup to start.

The "Find My" feature is prompted and activated the moment you sign in with your Apple ID during the iPhone SE 2020 setup. "Find My" is an app that locates your iPhone, AirPods, Apple Watch, connected family and friends, and other iOS related devices.

The "Find My" app contains a feature named "Activation Lock" that prohibits anyone else from activating or using your iPhone SE 2020, even if the iPhone is totally erased. If you decide to sell or give away your iPhone device, ensure that you erase and unlock the activation lock so that the next owner will be able to activate it.

Using the iPhone On Other Cellular Networks

A few carriers allow you to open the iPhone for use with other carriers, i.e. to contact your carrier for approval and arrangement data. In order to finish the process, there must be an already established link between the iPhone and iTunes account, however extra expenses may apply.

Connecting to the Internet

iPhone connects to the Internet at whatever point using an accessible Wi-Fi connection or your iPhone's cellular data. At the point when an Internet connection is required, the iPhone SE 2020 connects to the most accessible Wi-Fi in range, showing a rundown of the closest Wi-Fi networks.

Making a Wi-Fi Connection

If the Wi-Fi symbol shows up at the top of your screen, it indicates that you're connected to a Wi-Fi network. Your iPhone SE 2020 reconnects to that network whenever you return to that location.

Configure Wi-Fi

In order to configure your iPhone's Wi-Fi, go to Settings the and proceed to click on the Wi-Fi option, you can either choose to turn the Wi-Fi on or off here.

Select a Network

Click on one of the listed Wi-Fi networks then input the password, if required. Enable "Ask to Join Network". This will be prompted whenever a Wi-Fi network is available within your range. If you do not enable this option, you will have to manually join a network where a previously connected Wi-Fi network isn't accessible.

To join a closed Wi-Fi network, click on the "Other" option and input the name of the network. You should know the network name, security type, and password.

Manipulate the Settings of a Wi-Fi Network

Select the information icon next to a network. You can renew the settings provided by the Dynamic Host Configuration Protocol server.

Forget a Wi-Fi Network

Click on the information symbol next to a Wi-Fi network you've joined before and proceed to select the "Forget This Network" option.

The iPhone SE 2020's Control center is a quick shortcut to make changes to your Wi-Fi connection. Various Wi-Fi options including turning on/off the Wi-Fi, searching for Wi-Fi networks nearby, connecting to a network can be done quickly in the control center.

Setting up Your own Wi-Fi Network

If you have an unconfigured AirPort base station enabled and within your district, you can make use of the iPhone to carry out the setup. All you need to do is go to Settings, proceed to the Wi-Fi option, search for "Set up an AirPort station", select "Your Base" and the setup assistant will handle the rest.

Managing an Airport Network

At the Settings page, select the Wi-Fi option and tap the information symbol beside the network name, proceed to select "Manage This Network". If you don't have the AirPort app installed on your iPhone, click "OK" to open the App Store, then download it (this will require an internet connection).

Setting Up Date and Time

The date and time are normally set for you based on your location information. View the iPhone Lock screen to check whether the stated date and time is precise.

To set and update the date and time automatically, go to Settings, then General, then to the Date and Time option. At that point, turn on the 'Set Automatically' feature. iPhone applies the right time over the cellular network system and updates it for the time zone you're in. A few network carriers don't encourage network time, so in certain zones, the iPhone will be unable to naturally decide the local time.

If you prefer to set the date and time manually, go to Settings, then General, then Date and Time to disable the 'Set Automatically' feature.

Another decision you might have to make when it comes to setting up date and time is whether to show 24-hour time or 12-hour time. To select your preferred method, go to Settings > General > Date and Time, at that point turn 24-Hour Time on or off (not accessible in all territories).

Setting Up Phone Language

Go to Settings > General > Language and Region to set:

- The language for iPhone
- The desired language for applications and sites
- The locale formats
- The calendar designs
- The temperature unit (Celsius or Fahrenheit)

To include a keyboard for another dialect, go to Settings > General > Keyboard > Keyboards.

Apple ID

Your Apple ID is the account under which you do everything with Apple. You are granted the ability to access all Apple services with just Apple ID and password.

Signing in With Your Apple ID

If you already have an Apple ID from previously using an iPhone, use it to check-in when you first set up your iPhone. On occasion, you need to access an Apple service. In a situation whereby you did not register in the course of setup, visit Settings > Sign into your iPhone.

If you don't have an Apple ID, you can create one when asked to sign in to use an Apple service. It's important to register for Apple ID.

An included feature of signing in with Apple ID is the "Sign in with Apple ID Privacy" option that gives you a helpful and data-safe approach to signing into applications and sites. Apple can even produce a one-time use randomized email address, so you never need to give your genuine email address away to an application again. Two-factor validation is incorporated with this element to give you significantly greater security.

Changing your Apple ID Settings

Visit the Settings page > [your name] to update your contact information, create a new password, and other vital information.

Setting up iCloud

Users can securely store photos, videos, and other files on iCloud. Files stored on iCloud are even available in case the users lose their iPhone SE 2020.

To set up your iCloud, simply sign in to the iCloud with your initially registered Apple ID. Files stored in iCloud are remotely linked to your other devices where you have the iCloud enabled by signing in with your Apple ID or with the Touch ID biometrics you have previously set up.

Alternatively, you can check in to iCloud through iCloud.com from any Mac or PC. This permits you to access your iCloud details and contents.

However, please note that iCloud features may be subjected to modifications depending on location.

Services iCloud offer includes:

Photos and Videos Storage

By utilizing the iCloud Photo Library to store your photos and videos, you can easily and securely access them from any iPhone device, Mac or your personal computer, if it has the iCloud for Windows installed (all dependent on certain operating system requirements). You can also sign into iCloud.com with your Apple ID on any of the aforementioned devices. One of the interesting features of iCloud is the "iCloud Photo Sharing" option which lets you share photos and videos with people selected by you and permits them to add photos, videos, and comments. If iCloud is your chosen and selected option when it comes to storing documents, you cannot use iTunes to synchronize your documents with your computer.

Documents Storage and Retrieval

When you save documents on the iCloud drive on the Files application, you can access them on any iPhone device.

Data Backup

You can back up your iPhone SE 2020 to iCloud automatically when your device is connected to a power source and a Wi-Fi network or an active cellular data network. iCloud contents shared over the Internet are encoded. Family Sharing permits you to share iCloud storage on plans with over two hundred gigabytes with about six family members.

Synchronization of mails, contacts, calendars, notes, reminders, and more, allows for constant updates across all your devices.

Keeping Tabs on your Internet Surfing

Find My iPhone

You can make use of the "Find My" app on another iOS device or utilize the Web application on any Mac or personal computer to locate your missing iPhone or other iOS devices linked to your iPhone on a map. You can then choose to lock the device remotely, block certain abilities such as paying using Apple Pay, play a sound of significant volume, display certain messages, or to wipe the device of every data it has on it.

The "Find My" feature also includes Activation Lock, which demands your Apple ID and password to disable the "Find My" feature, clear off the iPhone, or to reactivate your device.

The "Find My" app also lets you find friends and family that have shared their location with you.

Credit Card Information

Passwords and credit card details are kept by the iCloud keychain and it updates these regularly across all your designated devices.

The iCloud offers you a free email account with about five gigabytes of storage for your content and backups. You can purchase extra storage space from your device. Your purchased music, applications, television shows and books do not take up your available storage space.

Upgrading your iCloud Storage

To update your iCloud storage, visit the Settings page on your iPhone, proceed to the "Your Name" option, then select "iCloud " and choose the "Manage Space" option, then tap Upgrade.

Setting up Other Mails, Contacts and Calendar Accounts

To set up an account, visit Settings >Mail, Contacts, Calendar >Add Account.

Contacts can be added by utilizing the LDAP (Lightweight Directory Access Protocol) or CardDAV account provided your enterprise supports it

Calendars, on the other hand, are added using a CalDAV calendar and you can enhance the experience using iCalendar.

Migrating from Android to iOS

While setting up your iPhone, you can choose to transfer your files and important data automatically and safely from your android device.

A very important thing to do is to ensure that Wi-Fi is enabled on your android device or your android device is connected to a strong Wi-Fi network.

Ensure that your new iOS gadget and your Android gadget are plugged into a power source. Ensure that the data you're transferring, including the contents of your supplement Micro SD card, will fit on your new iOS gadget. If you need to move your Chrome bookmarks, update to the most recent version of Chrome on your Android gadget.

While you set up your new iOS gadget, search for the Apps and Data screen. At this point, select the "Move Data from Android" option. If you have initially completed your iPhone setup, you will be asked to erase your iOS device and begin from scratch. Perhaps you do not want to go through the stress of erasing your iPhone, you will be left with no other option than to transfer the contents manually.

Install and open the Move to iOS application and tap 'Continue'. It is advisable that you read through the terms and conditions. To proceed after reading the terms and conditions, tap the "Agree" button, then tap 'Next' in the upper right corner of the 'Find Your Code' screen.

On your iOS gadget, click 'Continue' on the screen called 'Move from Android' that will be displayed. At that point, all that's required of you is to wait for a ten-digit or six-digit code to show up. If, by contrast, your Android displays a cautionary message that you do not have a strong internet connection, you can disregard the caution and carry on. Enter the code on your Android gadget. Now, all you need to do is to hold on for the Transfer Data screen to be displayed.

Select the contents that you intend to transfer on your Android phone and click on the "Next" button. Regardless of whether your Android shows that the procedure is finished — leave the two gadgets alone until the loading bar that shows up on your iOS gadget is complete. The entire exchange can take some time, depending on how much content you're moving.

Here's what gets moved: contacts, message history, camera photographs and recordings, web bookmarks, mail records, and schedules. If they're accessible on both Google Play and the App Store, a portion of your free applications will move also. After the exchange finishes, you can download any free applications from the App Store.

Set up your iOS Gadget

After the loading bar completes on your iOS gadget, tap 'Done' on your Android gadget. At that point, tap 'Continue' on your iOS gadget and follow the onscreen steps to complete the setup for your iOS gadget.

Wrap Up

Ensure that the entirety of your android content is moved. Music, Books, and PDFs should be moved by transferring manually.

Making Synchronization and Backups

Managing content on your iPhone SE 2020 You can move information and files from an iPhone to another iOS device, Mac or another computer via either iCloud or iTunes.

iCloud keeps your pictures and videos, documents, music and much more. These files will be remotely linked to your other iOS devices as iCloud updates them. iTunes synchronizes music, videos, and much more between your computer and iPhone. Alterations made on one device are replicated on the other when you synchronize.

You can choose iCloud or iTunes, whichever you prefer.

Backup iPhone with iCloud Backup

After signing in with your Apple ID, iCloud backup is automatically enabled. iCloud backs up your iPhone data daily when locked and connected to a Wi-Fi and power source. Backups initiated by iCloud are encoded, giving you the satisfaction of data protection from unauthorized entries when data is being transmitted to your device or while it's being stored in iCloud. As already stated, when using the iCloud backup, you cannot make use of the iTunes backup.

However, iCloud backups do not include a couple of things:

- Initially stored data in iCloud
- Other cloud services stored such as Gmail and Exchange mail.
  Touch ID settings
- Apple Pay information and settings

- Contents from iTunes store app, App Store, or iBooks Store.

Stopping or Resuming iCloud Backups

Visit the Settings page > "Your Name" option >iCloud >iCloud Backup. Here, you can choose either to enable or disable the backup feature.

To back up your files promptly on iCloud, select the "Back Up Now" option in the iCloud section of the Setting page. To view or remove iCloud Backups, on the iCloud section, select "Manage Storage" >Backup, then select a backup from the list.

Synchronizing by Connecting your iPhone SE 2020 to your Computer

An alternative to synchronizing your iPhone using iTunes or the back up with the iTunes method is by connecting your iPhone to a computer.

You can also choose to synchronize with iTunes through wireless means. To link your iPhone with a computer, you need to meet certain requirements:

- A Mac equipped with a USB 2.0 or 3.0 port
- A Personal computer with a USB 2.0port Operating system X 10.9 or later
- Windows 7 or later
- iTunes 12.5 or later.

You can use the lightning to USB cable included in the phone box to connect the iPhone SE 2020 to your computer.

You can disconnect the iPhone from the computer anytime you need to. However, if the iPhone SE 2020 is actively synchronizing with your computer, do not disconnect it as this might result in some data not being synchronized until you next connect your iPhone with the computer. Whenever you are synchronizing with a computer, check the iTunes screen on your iPhone or computer to follow the progress of the synchronization.

Synchronizing With iTunes

This type of synchronization copies information from your computer to the iPhone, and the other way around. You can carry out this synchronization by connecting your iPhone to your computer or set up the iTunes to carry out a wireless Synchronization of music, videos, and other items with a Wi-Fi network connection.

For assistance with synchronizing, launch iTunes on your computer, choose the "Help" option >iTunes Help option >Show topics, then select the "Add items to iPod, iPhone or iPad" option.

To carry out synchronization with a USB cable, use the lightning to USB cable to connect the iPhone to your computer, launch iTunes on your computer, then click the iPhone button at the top left of the iTunes window. Go ahead to choose a setting to configure it.

If the iPhone doesn't appear in iTunes, and you are using the updated version of iTunes, inspect the cable to ensure proper connection, then restart your computer.

Setting Up Wireless Synchronizing

Use the lightning to USB cable to connect the iPhone to your computer, launch iTunes, then click the iPhone button at the top left of the iTunes window. Tap on the "Summary" option, select "Synchronize with this iPhone over Wi-Fi"

Provided that Wi-Fi synchronizing is turned on, and both the iPhone and the computer are active and linked to the same wireless network, the iPhone should Synchronize when connected to a power source if iTunes is open.

iTunes provides you with several synchronizing options: -With Music, you can choose to synchronize your whole music library or just one playlist, album, artist or genre. -As for Movies, Television Shows, Podcasts, and Books pages, you can synchronize the entire media contained in them or just the files selected by you.

-With Photos, you can synchronize photos and videos from some selected and trusted apps or folders on your personal computer.

You can enable iTunes to automatically synchronize the iPhone when it's linked to your computer. You can also choose to prevent this automated synchronization by utilizing the "Hold command" option on Mac, or shift + control button on the PC until the iPhone is displayed at the top of the iTunes window.

Backing Up your iPhone SE 2020 with iTunes

Launch the iTunes application on your computer, then connect your iPhone device to your computer. When the iPhone icon shows up on the computer, click on the icon, then click "Summary" in the side panel.

To activate manual backup, the "Backup Now" option is the most appropriate to choose from. However, if your choice is to activate an automatic iTunes backup, then "This Computer" would be the correct option to choose. iTunes automatically backs up the iPhone when it is connected to your computer.

To backup Activity, Health and Keychain data on iTunes, you can select the "Encrypt Local Backup" option in iTunes. However, backing up on iTunes doesn't include:

- Contents bought from iTunes Store, App Store, Portable Document Formats downloaded directly into iBooks
- Items synchronized from iTunes
- Photos already stored in the cloud as in iCloud
- Shared Streams, My Photo Stream, and iCloud Photo Library.
- Your Touch ID set preferences
- Apple Pay information and preferences

Encrypting iPhone SE 2020 Backups

Encoding backups made on your iPhone by iTunes which are stored on your computer involves selecting the "Encrypting iPhone backup" option in the summary pane. Encrypted backups are characterized by a lock icon and to recover the backup, you will require a password. Passwords for other activities are not contained in the backup, therefore, you have to input those passwords again if using backup to recover the iPhone.

Viewing or Removing iTunes Backups

Launch the iTunes application on your computer, select iTunes >Preferences, then select the "Devices" option. Encoded backups show a lock icon in the list of backups.

When you replace your iPhone, backup is what you can make use of to transfer your information to a new device.

Chapter Three

Home Screen

The Home Screen displays all the applications you have installed on your iPhone SE 2020. It includes multiple pages which are added as you download more applications.

To get to the home screen from any page you are on, press the home button. To see more of your applications when you're on the home page, swipe right or left on the home screen pages.

Some installed applications may display a notifications badge on their home screen icon to inform you about the number of notifications that await you.

To open/launch an app while you're on the home screen tap the app icon.

Gestures on the iPhone SE 2020

You can utilize a few gestures such as tap, drag, swipe, and pinch to control the iPhone and the applications installed on it. When you launch an app and you want to look around, drag the list of items in the upward direction or the downward direction to see more and explore the application. To immediately return to the top of a page, tap the status bar that is displayed at the top of the screen.

To zoom a photo, web page, or Maps page, pinch out on the page to zoom in and pinch in to zoom out. In the Photos app, pinching in on a photo returns you to the collection in which the picture is contained. An alternative method to zooming in on an item is by double-tapping on the item. The first double-tap zooms in on the item, and the preceding double-tap zooms it out. In Maps, if you double-tap and hold the page, you can then drag up to zoom in or drag the page down to zoom out.

A Haptic Touch is a touch and hold feature on the iPhone. Haptic Touch can be utilized by pressing an important area until a somewhat haptic pop is felt against the finger and an optional menu springs up, with content differing, depending on where you're utilizing the feature. You can utilize it on Home screen application symbols to raise Quick Actions. You can utilize it on links, telephone numbers, locations, and more to review content or to enact various gestures on the iPhone or raise different menus.

The haptic touch setting is situated in the Accessibility area of the Settings application:

Open the Settings application.

Pick the Accessibility area.

Tap on "Contact."

Tap on "Haptic Touch."

Status Icons

Status icon		What it means
▗▖▄▐	Cell signal	You're in range of the cellular network and can make and receive calls. If there's no signal, "No service" appears.
✈	Airplane mode	Airplane mode is on—you can't make phone calls, and other wireless functions may be disabled. See Travel with iPhone.
LTE	LTE	Your carrier's LTE network is available, and iPhone can connect to the Internet over that network. (Not available in all areas.) See Cellular data settings.
4G	UMTS	Your carrier's 4G UMTS (GSM) or LTE network (depending on the carrier) is available, and iPhone can connect to the Internet over that network. (Not available in all areas.) See Cellular data settings.
3G	UMTS/EV-DO	Your carrier's 3G UMTS (GSM) or EV-DO (CDMA) network is available, and iPhone can connect to the Internet over that network. See Cellular data settings.
E	EDGE	Your carrier's EDGE (GSM) network is available, and iPhone can connect to the Internet over that network. See Cellular data settings.
GPRS	GPRS/1xRTT	Your carrier's GPRS (GSM) or 1xRTT (CDMA) network is available, and iPhone can connect to the Internet over that network. See Cellular data settings.
Wi-Fi	Wi-Fi call	iPhone is set up for Wi-Fi calling. iPhone also displays a carrier name next to the icon. See Make a call.
📶	Wi-Fi	iPhone is connected to the Internet over a Wi-Fi network. See Connect to Wi-Fi.
◉	Personal Hotspot	iPhone is providing a Personal Hotspot for another device. See Personal Hotspot.
↻	Syncing	iPhone is syncing with iTunes. See Sync with iTunes.

Navigation Bar and Toolbar Icons

☀	**Network activity**	Shows that there's network activity. Some third-party apps may also use it to show an active process.
☏→	**Call Forwarding**	Call Forwarding is set up. See Call forwarding, call waiting, and caller ID.
VPN	**VPN**	You're connected to a network using VPN. See VPN settings.
☏	**TTY**	iPhone is set to work with a TTY machine. See Support for TTY.
🔒	**Lock**	iPhone is locked. See Lock screen.
🌙	**Do Not Disturb**	Do Not Disturb is turned on. See Do Not Disturb.
🔄	**Portrait orientation lock**	The iPhone screen is locked in portrait orientation. See Change the screen orientation.
➤	**Location Services**	An item is using Location Services. See Location Services.
⏰	**Alarm**	An alarm is set. See Set an alarm or bedtime schedule.
✳	**Bluetooth®**	*Blue or white icon:* Bluetooth is on and paired with a device. *Gray icon:* Bluetooth is on. If iPhone is paired with a device, the device may be out of range or turned off. See Bluetooth devices.
🎧	**Headphones connected**	iPhone is paired with Bluetooth headphones that are turned on and within Bluetooth range. See Bluetooth devices.
🔋	**Bluetooth battery**	Shows the battery level of a paired Bluetooth device.
🔋	**Battery**	*Gray icon:* Shows the iPhone battery level or charging status. See Charge and monitor the battery. *Yellow icon:* Low Power Mode is on. See Low Power Mode.

◀◀	Rewind	Moves backwards through media playback or slides.	rewind
Save	Save	Saves the current state.	save
Q	Search	Displays a search field.	search
X	Stop	Stops media playback or slides.	stop
🗑	Trash	Deletes the current or selected item.	trash
Undo	Undo	Undoes the last action.	undo

Icon	Name	Meaning	API
⬆️	Action (Share)	Shows a modal view containing share extensions, action extensions, and tasks, such as Copy, Favorite, or Find, that are useful in the current context.	action
+	Add	Creates a new item.	add
📖	Bookmarks	Shows app-specific bookmarks.	bookmarks
📷	Camera	Takes a photo or video, or shows the Photo Library.	camera
Cancel	Cancel	Closes the current view or ends edit mode without saving changes.	cancel
✏️	Compose	Opens a new view in edit mode.	compose
Done	Done	Saves the state and closes the current view, or exits edit mode.	done
Edit	Edit	Enters edit mode in the current context.	edit
⏩	Fast Forward	Fast-forwards through media playback or slides.	fastForward
📁	Organize	Moves an item to a new destination, such as a folder.	organize
⏸	Pause	Pauses media playback or slides. Always store the current location when pausing, so playback can resume later.	pause
▶️	Play	Begins or resumes media playback or slides.	play
Redo	Redo	Redoes the last action that was undone.	redo
↻	Refresh	Refreshes content. Use this icon sparingly, as your app should refresh content automatically whenever possible.	refresh
↩️	Reply	Sends or routes an item to another person or location.	reply

◀◀	Rewind	Moves backwards through media playback or slides.	rewind
Save	Save	Saves the current state.	save
Q	Search	Displays a search field.	search
X	Stop	Stops media playback or slides.	stop
🗑	Trash	Deletes the current or selected item.	trash
Undo	Undo	Undoes the last action.	undo

Home Screen Quick Action Icons

Icon	Name	Meaning	API
+	Add	Creates a new item.	add
⏰	Alarm	Sets or displays an alarm.	alarm
🔊	Audio	Denotes or adjusts audio.	audio
📖	Bookmark	Creates a bookmark or shows bookmarks.	bookmark
📷	Capture Photo	Captures a photo.	capturePhoto
🎥	Capture Video	Captures a video.	captureVideo
☁	Cloud	Denotes, displays, or initiates a cloud-based service.	cloud
✎	Compose	Composes new editable content.	compose
✓	Confirmation	Denotes that an action is complete.	confirmation
👤	Contact	Chooses or displays a contact.	contact
📅	Date	Displays a calendar or event, or performs a related action.	date
★	Favorite	Denotes or marks a favorite item.	favorite
🏠	Home	Indicates or displays a home screen. Indicates, displays, or routes to a physical home.	home
↓	Invitation	Denotes or displays an invitation.	invitation
➤	Location	Denotes the concept of location or accesses the current geographic location.	location

	Love	Denotes or marks an item as loved.	love
	Mail	Creates a Mail message.	mail
	Mark Location	Denotes, displays, or saves a geographic location.	markLocation
	Message	Creates a new message or denotes the use of messaging.	message
	Pause	Pauses media playback. Always store the current location when pausing, so playback can resume later.	pause
	Play	Begins or resumes media playback.	play
	Prohibit	Denotes that something is disallowed.	prohibit
	Search	Enters a search mode.	search
	Share	Shares content with others or to social media.	share
	Shuffle	Indicates or initiates shuffle mode.	shuffle
	Task	Denotes an uncompleted task or marks a task as complete.	task
	Task Completed	Denotes a completed task or marks a task as not complete.	taskCompleted
	Time	Denotes or displays a clock or timer.	time
	Update	Updates content.	update

Switching Between Applications on iPhone SE 2020

While you are active on an application on the iPhone, you can easily switch to another application. To do this you double-click the Home button so that your open apps page is displayed in the app switcher. To see more apps that are open in the app switcher, swipe right or left and tap on the application you want to switch to.

To close or quit an app, double-click the home button to bring up the app switcher and you swipe on the app you intend to close.

Adjusting Volume Levels

Perhaps you're on the phone or listening to music and melodies, films, or other media, the buttons on the side of the iPhone can change the sound volume. Furthermore, the buttons control the volume for the ringer, alerts, and other audio cues. You can use Siri to crank the volume up or down by simply saying "increase the volume" or "turn down the volume."

Locking Ringer and Alert Volumes

Visit the Settings page >Sound and Haptics, then disable the "Change with the button" feature. To place a limit on the volume for music and videos, while you are in the settings page > Music > Volume limit. Also, you can place a limit on the maximum headset volume by going to the music section on the settings page >Volume settings > General >Restrictions >Volume Limit.

You can also make use of the iPhone Control Center on your iPhone to alter the volume level whenever your iPhone is locked or you are active on another app. Simply open the

Control Center, then drag the volume slider to whichever level you intend.

You might want to temporarily silence calls, notifications or alerts coming into your iPhone. You can do this by using the "Do Not Disturb" feature. You do this by going to the Control Center, then clicking on the crescent moon icon to enable or disable Do Not Disturb on your iPhone.

You can, however, choose to allow calls even when the "Do Not Disturb" feature is enabled. To permit incoming calls from selected contacts, tap the "Allow Calls From" option. To permit for repeated calls to come through in case of an emergency, enable the "Repeated Calls" option.

To allow calls and messages from emergency contacts when Do Not Disturb is enacted, go to Settings, choose a contact > Edit >Text Tone or Ringtone then enable "Emergency Bypass", or set up a Medical ID and indicate an emergency contact so that calls and messages come in from such emergency contacts even when Do Not Disturb is on.

To schedule the hours or moment for Do Not Disturb to be enacted, go to settings >Do Not Disturb, then enable "Scheduled". You will then be required to set the starting and stoppage time for your quiet hours.

Furthermore, you are permitted to set the instances when Do Not Disturb comes into play on your iPhone either when the iPhone is locked or unlocked. Put your iPhone in ring mode or silent mode by flipping the silent switch.

Set your Vibration Pattern

Visit Settings>Sound and Haptics, then select an item from the Sounds and Vibration Patterns list. To create yours, tap Vibration.

Using Do Not Disturb While Driving

Go to Settings > Do Not Disturb > Activate, then choose: Automatically (when iPhone assumes you are driving), Manually (just from Control Center), or when connected to Car Bluetooth.

If you select Manually, include Do Not Disturb While Driving at the Control Center. Go to Settings > Control center > Customize Controls, then tap and close Do Not Disturb While Driving.

When Do Not Disturb While Driving is turned on, it will activate when you are travelling. To continue getting calls, messages, and alerts while riding, tap the Do Not Disturb notice on the Lock screen, at that point tap 'I'm Not Driving'. Or press the Home button and tap 'I'm Not Driving'.

To send a programmed reply that you are driving, visit Settings >Do Not Disturb >Autoreply To, then select contacts or groups. To send a programmed reply to anyone whom you've sent messages to in the past two days, choose the "Recent" option.

To change the programmed auto-reply message for the Do Not Disturb feature, at the Auto-Reply section, tap Message to display the keyboard.

Lock Screen

The iPhone SE 2020 lock screen comes up when you switch the phone on or wake the iPhone. The lock screen offers you swift access to features and information that are important to you, even while the iPhone is locked.

Features Lock Screen Offers

See your latest notifications. To access notifications from the previous day, swipe in the upward direction from the center of the screen.

You can open the camera by swiping towards the left direction on the lock screen.

Swiping right on the lock screen enables you to access "Today View" which displays information about your favorite applications at a glimpse

The lock screen leads you to the Control Center when you swipe up from the bottom corner. To unlock your iPhone, press the home button which has your Touch ID biometrics registered, an alternative is to enter your passcode if need be.

You are allowed to change what you can access from the lock screen by going to Settings >Touch ID and selecting Passcode. Here you can change access to a list of options of your choice.

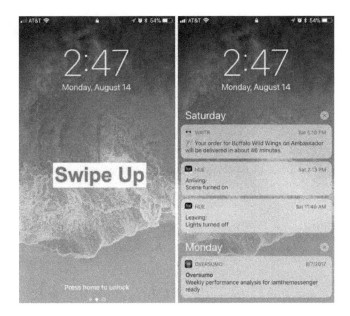

Notifications

Notifications updates and informs you of what's new or recent developments. It notifies you about a call you missed, a postponed event, and other information. You can manipulate your notifications so that it only notifies you about what's important to you.

To respond to a notification, simply tap it. If you are active on an application and you do not wish to visit the app in order to see the notification, drag down on the notification when it shows up at the crest of your screen.

To get rid of notifications without giving a response to them, swipe them up.

Swiping down from the top corner of the screen shows your latest notifications. In the same manner, swiping up from the center of the screen displays older notifications.

To cast off a notification from the notification panel, hold down on the notification and then tap the cancel icon (×).

Changing notification preferences can be done in the notification section in the settings page. Click on an app icon to choose whether or not to grant permission for notifications and to fix notification style options.

To change how previews will be displayed for all applications, select the "Show Preview" option, then select from a list of options.

To choose whether or not to display notifications on the lock screen, select Touch ID and Passcode in the Settings page, then underneath the "Allow Access When Locked" option, enable Recent Notifications.

Furthermore, you can enable government alerts in the Government Alert List on the Notifications section in the Settings page.

Moreover, if you choose to Silence your entire notifications, visit the Do Not Disturb section in the Settings page. You can use Siri to enable or disable the Do Not Disturb feature by saying " Enable Do Not Disturb" or "Disable Do Not Disturb".

Control Center

Control center on the iPhone SE 2020 grants you access to a bunch of handy features.

To access the Control Center, swipe up from the bottom corner of your 4.7-inch screen. A significant portion of the status icons that will be exhibited to you offers further options. To connect to a Wi-Fi network, tap on the Wi-Fi icon, holding on the Wi-Fi icon shows you further options such as the list of available networks. To disconnect from the current Wi-Fi network you're on, tap on the Wi-Fi icon and the Wi-Fi feature will be disabled. The same process applies to the Bluetooth feature and other features in the control center.

To close the control center on iPhone SE 2020, swipe down the screen or click on the home button. You can hinder access to the control center in applications in the settings page. Furthermore, you can customize controls in the Control Center. To do this, move to the Control Center section in the settings page and proceed to customize controls. Tap the add+ or eliminate- icons to modify controls and also move the controls to a new position.

Manipulating the Screen Orientation

Many installed and programmed applications on the iPhone SE 2020 will exhibit a different view when you rotate the phone. In landscape mode, a number of applications have a unique layout, these areas are Mail, Calendar, Settings, and Messages.

To lock the screen orientation and prevent it from rotating anytime it senses gravitational change, access the control center and tap the portrait orientation lock icon. The portrait orientation lock icon appears in the status bar when the screen orientation is sealed.

Chapter Four

Typing and Editing Texts

Tap on the text box for the onscreen keyboard to be displayed, then tap the letters to type. Should an incorrect letter come up, you can swipe your finger to the appropriate letter.

Typing in Uppercase

To achieve this, tap the shift key and tap a letter to enable caps-lock, double-tap the shift key.

Tapping on the numeric keys or symbol keys inputs numbers, symbols, and even punctuations into the text box. Inputting an accented or alternate character involves touching and holding a key, then sliding to choose one of the displayed options.

To quickly put an end to a sentence, double-tap the Spacebar.

Keyboard Assistive Functions:

Swipe Typing

The Swipe Typing feature enables you to quickly type long sentences by swiping and sliding across letters on the keyboard.

Corrective Spelling

The iPhone SE 2020 keyboard has an embedded spell checker. Whenever a word typed by you is underlined in red, tap it to see the proposed corrections. If the word you want to see doesn't come up, input the correction.

One-hand Typing

One-hand typing enables you to move the keyboard nearer to your thumb. To do this, touch and hold the smiley emoticon or web icon on the keyboard, then swipe to pick one of the keyboard layouts.

The iPhone SE 2020's onscreen keyboard features more keys when you orientate the iPhone to landscape.

To dictate words as opposed to typing, the wireless keyboard is the preferred option.

Revising texts demands you touch and delay your touch on the text to zoom the text and drag the situate the point of input.

Text Selection

Tap on the input point to reach a list of options. An alternative method is to double-tap to select it. Drag the grab points across the field to select the text. In documents that have been coded into the read-only mode, touch and hold on a piece of text to select it.

Other options made available to you over selected texts are cut, copy, or paste. With the aid of universal clipboard, you can use these options to interact between two Apple devices. That is, you can cut or copy texts on one Apple device and paste it on another.

The drag and drop option permit you to move selected texts within an application. Certain applications grant you further options for a selected piece of text such as to make a text bold, italicized, or underlined. You can view suggestions in Look Up or involve Siri to provide alternatives to the text.

Predictive Text

As you input your texts, Siri predicts what it thinks will be your next word, suggests emojis, and proposes other ideas depending on your recent activity and information.

Tap a suggested text to input it or accept a highlighted prediction by inputting a space or symbol. Space appears behind a suggested word when you tap it, then at the moment you type in a comma, full stop or any punctuation of your choice, space is erased. However, if your choice is to reject a suggestion, simply tap on the original word you inputted.

Disabling Predictive Text

Delay your touch on the smiley emoji or Web icon by swiping to keyboard settings and disabling predictive text. Even when the predictive text feature has been disabled, the iPhone might still try to propose corrections if any misspelling is detected. To decline a correction, tap the "X" option. If you keep on declining a specific correction, the iPhone will cease to bring it up.

Dictated Texts

Provided the Dictated Text Feature has been enabled in the keyboard section of the Settings page, you can use dictated texts rather than type them. Using dictated text doesn't require an Internet connection.

To dictate text, tap the microphone icon situated on the onscreen keyboard and then speak into it. After you have spoken into it, tap Done.

Tap to begin dictation.

Saving Keystrokes

A bypass permits you to enter a text or a phrase by inputting just a few characters. For instance, input "OMW" to enter "On My Way" and countless types that you can add by yourself.

Including and Changing Keyboards

You can turn inputting features, for example, spell checking, on or off. You can include keyboards for writing in various dialects and convert the format of your onscreen keyboard display.

On the off chance that you've included keyboards in different languages, your keyboard will switch between the two dialects you use often.

Set Input Features

Delay your touch on the smiling emoji or Web icon, then move to Keyboard settings. Otherwise, go to Settings, select General > Keyboard.

Adding a keyboard for an alternative dialect: Go to Settings, move to General, then to keyboard> then select Add New Keyboard.

Switching keyboards is done by holding on the smiling emoji or web, then swipe your finger to the keyboard's name. You can also tap the smiling emoji or Web to change from one keyboard to the next. Keep on tapping to get to other keyboards.

Chapter Five

Moving Items and Files on the iPhone SE 2020

Utilizing the drag and drop feature, you can use your finger to move items within an application. With this, you can reorder a list in the Reminders app and so on. However, please note that not all third-party apps support the drag and drop feature.

To move an item, touch and hold until it is lifted, then drag it to another position within the application. If what you're dragging is in a long document, then you have to drag it to the crest or bottom. It should automatically scroll, however, if what you are moving is a text, you have to select it first before dragging.

You can move multiple items at the same time. To do this, you touch and hold on the first item and while still holding on the screen, drag gently along the path of the items you intend to move. A badge exhibits the number of items that have been selected. You can then hold and drag all items together.

The Search Feature

When searching on the iPhone SE 2020, you obtain results from the Internet, iTunes and App Store and applications installed on your phone. You can personalize the applications you want to be included in the search results. An alternative to this is to use Siri to choose the applications by tapping Siri suggestions off or on in the settings page.

Searching with iPhone

To display Search from the Home Screen, swipe down from the screen's center. To display Search from an app, swipe down from the crest edge of the screen, then slide towards the right direction on the screen.

To conceal the keyboard and have access to additional results on the screen, tap search.

To open or launch a suggested application, tap on the application.
To explore more information about a search option, click on it, then tap one of the results to explore it.

To initiate a new search, tap × in the search box.

Disable Location Services for Suggestions

Visit the Settings page and proceed to privacy turn to Location Services. Select the "System Services" option, then disable Location-Based Suggestions.

A variety of applications include a search box in them so you can locate an item within the app. An example is the Maps app in which you can search for a particular location.

Using Mark-up

In certain applications including, Notes, Mail, and iBooks, you can elucidate images, notes, Portable Digital Formats (PDFs), and more. In other applications, you are permitted to add texts, speech bubbles, and other signatures and shapes.

To mark up an item, click on the encircled pen icon and draw with your finger. If it involves a screenshot, select the thumbnail that shows for a brief time in the bottom-left side of the screen.

To pick a tool that you will utilize for marking up, tap the pencil, pen, or marker tool, and change to the eraser in case of a mistake.

Move drawings by tapping the dotted rope-like circle, then drag the drawings and move your selected item to a new position.

Another choice you are at liberty to make is viewing extra color choices. Tap the present color to view more colors or orientate the iPhone to landscape.

Tap the add icon, then tap text. In the text box, select the Edit option and input your text. To alter the style or layout, tap AA. The text box can also be moved by dragging it about. At this point, tap Signature and Shape to input your signature and different shapes respectively.

To embed a shape with color or change how thick the lines are, tap the shape icon. To manipulate the form of a shape, drag the dot attached to the shape. Other options such as duplicating and deleting the shape are also made available to you.

To magnify a portion on the screen, tap the add icon, then select the magnifier. Move the green dot to alter the magnification level and the blue dot to adjust the magnifier's size.

Voice Control

Rather than conversing with Siri, you can utilize the Voice Control to make calls and control certain activities on the iPhone SE 2020. Moreover, you may want to use Voice Control in a situation where you can't make use of Siri because you do not have an Internet connection. When Voice Control is enacted, you can't converse with Siri.

To activate Voice Control, Go to Settings proceed to General >Accessibility then select Home Button, at this point, pick Voice Control.

To put the Voice Control into use, press and hold on the home button of the iPhone until the moment when the Voice Control screen comes up. Another alternative is to press and hold the center button of the headset.

For you to obtain optimum results from using voice control, you need to speak clearly and with a natural tone, utter only commands, names, and numbers exclusive to voice control commands and have a slight pause between statements, also ensuring that you utter full names.

You are required to utter voice commands in the language fixed for your iPhone. You can access information about these in the Language and Region section in the Settings page.

To disable Voice Control, on the same page where you turned it on, choose Siri or off. You can restrict Voice Control from dialing contacts when the iPhone is locked. Visit the Touch ID and Passcode section in the settings page and disable voice dial.

Chapter Six

Charging and Observing the Battery

The iPhone SE 2020 has an internal, lithium-ion rechargeable battery. To charge the battery, connect the iPhone to a power outlet utilizing the included cable and USB power adapter. An alternative method of charging the iPhone SE 2020 is by placing it face up on a Qi wireless charger and the battery will charge through wireless charging.

A precautionary measure and advice is to avoid using the lightning connector to charge the phone if it has come in contact with liquid as this may lead to electrocution.

Furthermore, you can charge the battery by connecting the iPhone SE 2020 to your computer. This also grants you passage to synchronize your iPhone with iTunes.

However, the iPhone's battery may be used up or diminished if connected to a computer that is not switched on or a computer put on standby mode.

To include the battery's percentage in the status bar, go to Settings > Battery > Turn on battery percentage. To view the rate at which each app consumes the battery, also check the Battery section in settings.

The battery icon in the crest-right edge of the iPhone displays the battery level or charging status. Charging the battery will amount to a longer time if you are synchronizing or using the iPhone SE 2020 while charging it.

A crucial point to note is that if the iPhone is significantly low on power, you may need to charge it for about ten minutes before you can make use of the phone. In a case where the battery is extremely down on power, the battery display may show up as blank for almost two minutes before the low battery image comes up.

Rechargeable batteries, like those embedded in the iPhone SE 2020, are provided with a certain amount of charge cycles and after a long period of time, it might need to be replaced. Battery replacements should be carried out by Apple or a competent service provider.

Low Power Mode

Change to Low Power Mode whenever your iPhone battery is on the downside or at moments when you may not have electricity provided in your domain.

This mode restricts background activities and restricts performance for certain tasks.

Enabling Low power mode can considerably extend the life of the battery.

You enable low power mode in the Battery section of the settings page. Once you charge the battery up to 80%, low power mode will be disabled and the normal power mode enabled.

Chapter Seven

Find My Application (Find My Friend)

The "Find My Friend" feature is made available to users in the "Find My" application on the iPhone SE 2020. This feature offers you a great method of sharing your location with people who are close to you.

Friends and relatives who share information about their location with you show up on a map, so you can access their present location.

You can also enable notification for such people so that you're alerted whenever they leave their locations or arrive at their destination.

Turn on Share My Location

In Settings, select "Your Name", then "iCloud", then choose "Share My Location".

Share Your Location with a Friend.

Launch the Find My application on your iPhone and tap on the "People" tab. Initiate the process of sharing your location by selecting the "Share My Location" option.

Proceed to input the name or telephone number of the individual or contact you intend to share your location information with and tap 'Send'.

A list of options will be provided for you from which you can choose to share your location just an hour, until the end of that particular day, or share indefinitely.

In return, when you share your location with somebody, they are provided with the choice to share their location.

Tag your Location

If it suits you, you can name the areas that you habitually visit. Launch the Find My application, proceed to select the "Me" tab. Move to the downward part of the page and pick Edit Location Name.

You will be provided with a list of places that you can choose from or go ahead to pick the "Add Custom Label" which offers you the ability to input any tag you have in mind for your area. Simply input the name of your choice and select 'Done'.

You can also use another device for your location sharing in the Find My app. To do this, go to the 'Me' tab and select the 'Use this to share my location' option.

Request to follow somebody's Location

To begin following someone else, you have to initially share your location with them. At that point, follow these means:

Open the Find My application and proceed to select the 'People' option. From there, pick the individual with whom you want to share your location.

Look down at the screen and tap on "Ask to Follow Location".

React to Location Sharing Solicitation

At the point when somebody shares their location with you, you can decide to reciprocate by also sharing yours. Launch the Find My application on your iPhone and select "People,". Below the name of the individual who recently shared with you their location, tap Share.

If you would prefer not to share your location to that individual, select Cancel.

Getting a Pick on a Friend's Location.

Launch the "Find My" application on your iPhone and proceed by selecting the People tab. Below this option, make a choice of the name of your friends who are in the same way sharing their location with you.

Pick the "Directions" options, picking this leads to the Maps being opened and thereafter follows the headings to show up at your Friend's area.

If your personal location shows up beneath your friend's name, it implies that you aren't following them. If you see the No Area Found statement, it denotes that the individual can't be found.

Additional things you can do with the Find My Application

At the point when you launch the Find My application, select the People tab, then pick the name of an individual. You are given a list of options which lets you:

- Have access to the contact card.
- Explore the person's location on maps.
- Add the individual to your list of Favorites or remove them. Individuals from Family Sharing can't be expelled from your list of Favorites.
- Select Edit Location Name to mark and tag their area.

However, to put an end to sharing your location, scroll down in the application, and select the option Stop Sharing My Location.

Travelling with iPhone

In situations whereby you travel outside your Carrier's network district, you can restrict roaming charges by disabling voice and data roaming services in the Cellular Data section in Settings.

Certain airline services grant you the freedom of leaving your iPhone switched on, provided you activate the "Airplane Mode". This implies that you will not be able to make calls or use the Bluetooth feature on the iPhone and by implication, restricting you to just being able to play games, listen to music, watch movies or make use of other applications that do not depend on network services to function.

To activate Airplane Mode, bring up the iPhone Control Center and tap the airplane icon. An alternative method of activating the Airplane Mode is by selecting it in the settings page.

Chapter Eight

Siri

Siri is a virtual helper that is a piece of Apple's AI. The assistant allows for voice inquiries and commands, and an inbuilt language UI responds to questions, makes proposals, and performs activities by assigning tasks to internet services. The results are improved with time and adjust to users' searches and inclinations.

The onscreen reaction from Siri frequently incorporates data or pictures that you can tap to access more information or make a further move.

To turn Hey Siri on or off, go to Settings > Siri and Search > Listen for "Hey Siri."

Furthermore, you can activate Siri with the home button. To do this, you are required to press and delay your hold on the home button, then release it at that point to make your inquiries known to Siri. Or, on the other hand, rather than hanging tight for Siri to sense that you've quit talking, let off your hold on the home button when you are done speaking.

Discover what Siri can do.

Ask Siri "what would you be able to do," or tap the question mark icon.

Enacting Corrections

In a situation whereby Siri misunderstands you or doesn't grasp your request, you can make corrections by either making a more verbally clarified inquiry or spelling such a word out for Siri.

Siri's Translation

Siri has the capability of translating written text from one foreign language into another. For instance, you can translate from English to Chinese, Italian, French, German, Mandarin, or Spanish.

Interacting with Siri

While interacting with Siri you can decide to change the voice gender in which Siri responds by going to "Siri and search" in the Settings page and proceeding to Siri Voice.

If you find out that Siri's response volume is low or too high, you can adjust the loudness using your iPhone's volume buttons. Another important aspect of interacting with Siri is whether or not to permit access to Siri when the iPhone SE 2020 is locked or deny access. This setting can be changed in Siri's sections of the settings page by selecting "Allow Siri When Locked".

Gist Siri about Yourself

To make conversing with Siri easier and to enable it to carry out commands much faster, you can tell Siri about yourself such as your work address, residential address and certainly your relationship. Doing this paves a way for you to be offered personalized services by Siri, for instance, services like "Send a Message to my Wife".

Once you have filled out the information card in Contacts on your iPhone, move to Settings and select the Siri and Search option. There, you click on "My information", and select the information fields in order to fill in the appropriate responses. You can teach Siri some basics such as learning to pronounce your name correctly and telling it about your relationship.

Securely Synchronizing what Information Siri Has Access to on Your Apple Devices.

You can restrict what information Siri has access to on your device as everything about you on the iPhone stays encoded.

Siri's Proactive Intelligence

Siri gains additional knowledge from you and can some of the time envision what you need and make recommendations before you demand something or pose an inquiry. Your intimate and exclusive information, which is encoded and stays private, synchronizes over all your gadgets marked into iCloud. As Siri finds out more about you on one gadget, Siri improves your experience on your other gadgets. Depending on how you utilize your iPhone, Siri makes proposals for what you should do straight away.

Siri may help when you:

Make Email and Schedule Occasions

When you begin adding individuals to an email or schedule an occasion, Siri recommends the individuals you included in past messages, events, meetings, or occasions.

Get Calls

Perhaps you're given a call from an obscure number, Siri gives you suggestions as to who a caller might be, especially if the number is included in your previous messages.

Leave for an Event, Occasion or Meeting

If your scheduled occasion involves travel, Siri evaluates traffic conditions and tells you when to leave.

Type Text Messages

While texting, Siri can propose names of motion pictures, places, and anything you came across recently. If you tell a companion you're on your way to a location, Siri can even propose your evaluated time of arrival.

Search in Safari

Siri makes proposals based on what you were browsing.

Confirm an Arrangement or a Book Trip on a Travel

Siri enquires as to whether you need to add it to your schedule.

Browse News Stories

As Siri uses AI to determine what stories you may be interested in.

More instances of how you can utilize Siri with applications show up all through this guide.

Siri and Applications

When it comes to your music taste, Siri can become your personal Disk Jockey since Apple Music knows your preferences. So, when you request Siri to play some music, you'll hear a tune you love. Siri can likewise reply to music-related questions like "Who's the drummer in this tune?"

Use Siri with outsider applications. Outsider applications, commonly referred to as third-party applications from the App Store support Siri. These applications allow you to book a ride, communicate something specific, search photographs, place calls, and trail your exercises. You can acquire more knowledge about applications that support Siri by searching for such applications in the App Store.

Disengaging Search and Siri Recommendations

Go to Settings then proceed to the "Siri and Search" option. At that point, disable Search and Siri recommendations for exclusive applications.

Siri Eyes Free

With this particular feature, you can utilize your iPhone while you are in your vehicle driving without having to make contact phone.

To converse with Siri, press and hold the voice order button on the directing wheel of your car until you hear the Siri tone. You can ask Siri to call individuals, select and play music, make instant messages, get bearings, read your notifications, find schedules, view updates and more. Siri Eyes Free is accessible to certain cars.

Chapter Nine

Personalize Your iPhone SE 2020

This is a feature on the iPhone that allows you to customize the display of the device however you like.

Arranging Your Programmed and installed Applications

To arrange your iPhone SE 2020, while on the home screen, touch and hold any application icon until the icon fidgets. When it does, drag the application to move it to a different side of the home screen.

In an instance whereby a particular home page is entirely occupied, you'll have to move the application to a different page. To do this, drag the app while holding on the home screen to the edge of the screen to trigger another home screen page to come up.

When you are done moving and arranging the application icons, press the home button on your iPhone SE 2020 to save your adjustment.

To view the number of home screen pages you have created, at the point of dragging an app towards the right edge of the home screen so as to move the app to a new page, check the number of dots above the dock which is situated at the lower part of the screen.

Restoring your Home Screen display to its Default Settings

Resetting your home screen layout causes the home screen applications to return to their default blueprint, and all folders made by you will be erased. To achieve this, visit the Settings page on your iPhone, tap on General then tap on Reset.

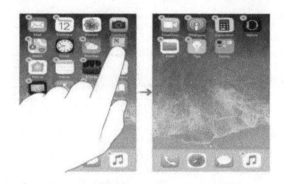

Make a Folder

When you put two or more applications on the home screen together, they become a folder. To set up a folder, touch and hold an application on the home screen until the icon fidgets and drag it into another app icon. Tap on the tag of the folder to rename it. To add more applications to the folder, drag the applications into it. To remove an application from a folder, drag the app out of the folder.

When you are done setting up the folder, press the home button. To clear off a folder from the home screen, all you need to do is hold it and it will be automatically deleted.

Remove Applications

To eliminate an application from the home screen, touch and hold the app icon while you're on the home screen until the icon fidgets. After you notice the fidgeting of the icon, tap ×, which is found at the upper-left side of the screen. When you are done affecting the removal of the app, press the home button.

Moreover, not only outsider applications can be removed, but certain manufacturer-programmed applications can also be removed, these applications are:

- Calculator-Calendar
- Compass
- Contacts: contacts' information remains intact and can be accessed through the phone app.
- FaceTime
- Files
- Find My Friends
- Home
- iBooks

- iCloud Drive
- iTunes Store
- Mail
- Maps
- Music
- News
- Notes
- Podcasts
- Reminders
- Stocks
- Tips
- TV
- Videos-Voice Memos
- Watch
- Weather

However, bear in mind that the removal of a built-in application by implication leads to any related user data and configuration files being erased. Also, eliminating built-in applications from your customized home screen can cause lags in the system's operation. Applications that are removed can be sought for and restored on the App Store.

Change Your Wallpaper

The wallpaper settings allow you to use pictures, which could be still images or dynamic images, as wallpapers for your home screen or your iPhone's lock screen. To change the present wallpaper, choose "Wallpaper" in Settings and then select Choose a New Wallpaper Option. While selecting a picture for wallpaper, you can enable the "perspective" option which prompts your wallpaper to move when you alter the orientation of the screen. To enable perspective in the Wallpaper section in Settings, tap on the icon of the lock screen.

Choose a live photo as your wallpaper by selecting the "Live Photo" option in the Settings page when you want to choose a new wallpaper.

Making Screen Brightness and Color Balance Adjustment

In a bid to save and extend battery life, make the screen dull and not illuminated in the control center. An alternative to this is to switch to Dark Mode which not only prolongs battery life but also makes viewing the screen easier on the eyes.

To adjust the level of screen brightness your phone offers, pull up the Control Center and adjust the "Screen brightness" bar and move the slider up or down to increase or reduce the screen's brightness respectively. An alternative method of doing this is in the "Display and Brightness" section in Settings which also gives you access to the slider.

To enact color balance adjustments, you need to enable the True Tone option which can be done in the "Display and Brightness" option in Settings. For your ease, pull up the

Control Center and tap on True Tone. It will show you the slider, then you either drag it to the warmer or cooler part of the spectrum. This is applicable to both the light mode and the dark mode.

Adjusting Screen Display (Dark mode)

Dark mode on the iPhone SE 2020 is a screen display option on its own. A large chunk of users prefer it because of the ease it offers when intending to operate under direct sunlight. It also brings screen reflections to the bare minimum. When you enable dark mode on your iPhone, it affects your screen display, theme, app background displays, and everything that used to have the normal display on your iPhone.

To enable dark mode, pull up the control center and tap on the dark mode icon. You can also enable the dark mode feature in the "Display and Brightness" option in the settings.

While you're on this page, you'll come across the "Option" toggle beneath the "Automatic" toggle. Both toggles provide you with a choice to switch between the Light mode and the Dark mode. The Option toggle leads you to two other options:

Sunset to Sunrise

This is the iPhone's originally programmed setting, which implies that the dark mode comes into play from sunset to sunrise, then the light mode comes back on.

Custom Schedule

Tapping on this allows you to manipulate the times when each mode of the display will be active. If you have set the dark mode to be enabled via the "Sunset to Sunrise" option, the iPhone makes use of data obtained from your clock and location services to distinguish between sunset and sunrise, ensuring that these features are enabled. You can enable Locations Services in the Privacy section in Settings.

Your iPhone Name

iTunes and iCloud utilize the name of your iPhone SE 2020. To fix a name or change the present name of your iPhone, go to Settings, then to General, select About, and then tap on the Name toggle.

App Restrictions

Certain applications permit you to augment the functionality of iPhone SE 2020. An app extension may be shown as a sharing option, a feature in Today View, default keyboard, or file provider. This extension aids you to adjust and filter a picture or video in your photos app. To get the app extension into your iPhone SE 2020, download it from App Store, then launch the application and follow the process which will be displayed onscreen when you are active on the application.

To enable or disable sharing or actions option.

Tap on the share icon, select more, and disable the third-party sharing. Normally this has been enabled by default. On this page, you can also choose to organize your sharing actions.

Set Restrictions

Restrictions can be placed on certain applications and items purchased online on the iPhone, for instance, one can choose to restrict certain features due to its explicit nature or prevent manipulations to certain settings. Furthermore, you can make use of this restriction feature of certain activities on the iPhone such as installation and utilization of certain applications, the maximum volume level, or manipulation of certain accounts.

To enable restrictions, go to Settings, select General, then tap the Enable Restrictions toggle. You will be required to state a restriction Passcode that's essential to effect the changes you make. This passcode does not necessarily have to be the passcode you choose for unlocking your iPhone. The important thing here is to ensure that you do not forget the passcode. If you do, you will be left with no other option than to restore the iPhone's software.

Chapter Ten

Sharing Items from Applications

Depending on the application you are using at that moment, tap on the Share toggle to choose the way you want to share your information in a number of applications. Extra options may be displayed on an application if the sharing option was used to download it. From the Files application, you can send any document by delaying your hold on the file icon and taping Share, then selecting the means with which you want the document to be sent.

Share Files From iCloud Drive

You can fine-tune files stored on your iCloud from any of your Apple gadgets with the aid of iCloud Drive. Any changes made on the Files appear on all your devices linked with iCloud Drive.

You can call on other people to view and amend a document by sharing a link to the document. You are expected to have signed into iCloud by using your Apple ID and have the iCloud Drive enabled to have access and use the iCloud Drive.

Enabling iCloud Drive is done by turning it on in the iCloud section in Settings.

Invite others to View or Edit a Document

The share toggle allows you to be exclusive about those you invite and permit to view and print documents you share with them and those that are prevented from making changes to the document.

Those you have also invited or given the link to the document and can view, print, and enact changes into the document depending on the rights you give them.

To enable this feature, tap the Browse option when you are in the Files app, then select iCloud Drive. Hold your touch on the document you intend to share, tap Share, and then click on the Add People toggle.

In the Share options, you can make decisions on which permission settings you want for the people you are sharing the documents to.

AirDrop

Airdrop lets you share pictures, videos, websites, locations and so on with other nearby Apple devices. AirDrop utilizes Bluetooth and Wi-Fi to share information. Both Wi-Fi and Bluetooth must be turned on and you need to sign in to your iCloud. Moreover, items transferred are encoded for security purposes.

To share items through AirDrop, with the Bluetooth and Wi-Fi on, tap on the Share icon, and proceed to tap on the name of a proximate AirDrop user. To receive items via AirDrop, turn on the hotspot feature in the Control Center of your iPhone, then choose whether to receive exclusively from contacts or from everyone.

Family Sharing

The Family Sharing feature permits about six members of a family to share iTunes Store, iBook Store, family photographs, family schedules, storage plans on iCloud, App Store, and lots more without the need to share an account.

To put family sharing into use, an adult will become the organizer, and make choices of features on behalf of the family to share, inviting up to five other family members to partake. At the time of joining, family sharing is activated automatically on other members' devices. Family Sharing requires your Apple ID to log in to your iCloud account. You are permitted to be in just one family group at a time.

To set up the family sharing feature, in the Settings page, click on Your Name toggle and then select Set Up Family Sharing. Follow the on-screen guides. Being a family organizer also demands that you deliberate on the features that you intend to share and make choices of members to invite. At some point, you will be instructed to create Apple accounts. If you decide to split certain Store purchases with members of your family, you accept to take care of the expenses they accrue at the moment of being members of the group.

The family sharing feature endows you with the option of creating an Apple ID for a child. Simply tap on the Create a Child Account toggle in the family sharing option.

Accepting an Invitation

Accepting an invitation on this feature is done by tapping Accept in your invitation toggle. An alternative to this is only useful when you are close to the organizer during the entire setup process, where you can input your sign in details on the organizer's device.

Sharing Purchases

Another option that family sharing offers is splitting purchases whenever members of your group, in other words, your family members, use any of the stores' purchase sharing options. All items are at the expense of the group organizer's Apple ID. As soon as an item is purchased, it is joined to the initiating Family member's account and is split among the other family members.

To gain access to information about purchases from any of the stores, launch the app and tap on Purchased toggle (or My Purchases toggle when referring to iTunes Store) and proceed to select a Family member. Members of the family can partake in the usage of a shared Apple Music Family Membership if the group has such a feature registered. This allows you to open Apple Music. Everyone in the group is entitled to their music playlist and personal music suggestions, however, be sure that you are duly signed in with your own Apple ID details.

Use a Shared iCloud Storage Plan

Depending on the iCloud storage capacity and plan, you can securely utilize as much storage capacity as you wish, and you can upgrade your storage plan should you require additional space.

Enable Ask Purchase

The family organizer, though somewhat being the head of the group, requires the other members to solicit for authorization for purchases or expense-free downloads. To do this, tap on the family member's name while you are in the Family Sharing section in Settings. There is an age restriction on this feature, but it varies with location.

Conceal Your Store Purchases

To conceal the whole of your purchases from other members of the family, in Family Sharing in Settings, input your name then disable the Share My Purchases option.

Share Media with Family Members

The moment you create Family Sharing, an album called Family Album is set up in the Photos app and will be present on the devices of respective all family members.

To share any form of media with other members, open the Photos app on your iPhone SE 2020, select the items you intend to share, tap the share icon, select iCloud photo sharing, input comments or captions and share to the group's family album. Members can unsubscribe from this feature, and the family organizer also has the authority to delete it.

Add Occasion to the Family Calendar

A shared calendar, tagged Family, is also created in the calendar app on the iOS device of every family member. To put up a family event, launch the calendar app, set up an event, and merge it to the occasion on the family calendar. Members can also unsubscribe from this, and the folder can be deleted by the organizer.

Enable Your Location to be Known by Other Family Members

This is activated by enabling the Share My Location feature in Settings. The Find My app also lets you trail the location of a family member. Another useful alternative to sharing your location is by using the Messages app to send your location. A useful application of sharing your location is that other family members can easily track your device if lost or stolen by using the Find My iPhone option in the Find My app.

Leave Family Sharing

Of course, you can choose to leave the group, this option is made available in the Family Sharing setup options in Settings. When you are on that page, tap Leave Family Sharing. However, if you happen to be the organizer, you can tap Stop Family Sharing to put an end to the group.

Chapter Eleven

Airplay Mirroring on iPhone SE 2020

Airplay is used to mirror your iPhone screen on Apple TV. Whenever the AirPlay Mirroring option is enabled, a blue bar shows up at the top of your iPhone screen. For your Airplay-enabled devices to be active when you tap on the mirror icon, ensure that all the devices are connected to the same Wi-Fi network.

To display the controls within AirPlay, pull up the Control Center and tap on Screen Mirroring. When you tap on Screen Mirroring, you are provided with a list of options from which you can choose the device that you intend to stream from.

To switch back to your iPhone SE 2020, tap on Screen Mirroring and turn off AirPlay mirroring. On the other hand, if you want to switch back to the iPhone from a streaming application, it follows the same process of tapping on Screen Mirroring, where you can then choose the iPhone.

With this feature and appropriate Apple cable, you will be able to link your iPhone SE 2020 to a television, projector, or any form of an external display gadget.

AirPrint

Just as the name sounds, AirPrint becomes useful when you require wireless printing from applications such as Mail, Safari,

Photos, and so on. Wireless printing is carried out on printers that are AirPrint enabled. The printer and the iPhone must be linked to the same Wi-Fi network.

Printing a Document

Depending on the application, tap on the Share icon. Scroll down through the list of options provided and tap Print. Move on to select the AirPrint-enabled printer. Proceed to choose which pages are to be printed, how many copies, the color of printed items, and lots more. When you are done making the selections, tap Print in the upper-right edge.

To view the status of items being printed, double-click on the Home button and tap on the Print center toggle. An icon will be displayed to you and the badge on the icon represents the number of items still in the queue. To revoke a Print job in progress, select the item in the Print center and tap Cancel Printing.

Apple EarPods

As stated earlier, you are provided with Lightning Connector EarPods in the phone's box. These EarPods have a built-in microphone, volume buttons, and a center button. The center is versatile and has a number of uses when connected to the iPhone SE 2020. It is used to control audio and video playbacks, receive and terminate calls, and also to summon Siri irrespective of the iPhone being locked or not.

In terms of controlling audio and video playback, the center button controls are highlighted below:

To interrupt a song or video, press the center button when the media is active. Press the button again to put an end to the interruption and return to the playback.

To move to the next song, press the center button twice quickly.

To go back to the previous song, press the center button three times consecutively and quickly.

To fast-forward, mainly when you are watching a video, press the center button swiftly two times and hold your touch on it.

To rewind a video you're watching, press the center button three times swiftly and hold your touch on it.

In terms of call management, the functions of the center button of the EarPods are highlighted below:

To receive an incoming call or terminate an ongoing call, simply press the center button.

To reject an incoming call, press and delay your hold on the center button for about two seconds, then release your hold. The slightly audible beep that sounds twice will confirm that you rejected the call.

Press the button when you are on a call to switch to another incoming call or a call that is being held. However, if you intend to terminate the current call and switch to an incoming call or a call that is being held, press and delay your hold on the button for about two seconds, then release your hold on the button. The faintly audible beep that sounds twice will confirm that you terminated the call.

To activate Siri via the EarPods center button, press and delay your hold on the center button until a beep sound is heard, then let go of your hold on the center button and make your inquiries known to Siri.

Apple Watch

The Apple Watch app on your iPhone is a perfect place to harness more knowledge about the Apple Watch. The application is also where you will link your iPhone SE 2020 to the Watch. To carry out this pairing, simply launch the Apple Watch app and go by the onscreen directions.

Apple Wireless Keyboard

The Apple Wireless Keyboard, which is an entity available on its own, is useful to input text on the iPhone. The keyboard is linked via Bluetooth, therefore, you must have initially paired the keyboard with your iPhone SE 2020.

Pair an Apple Wireless Keyboard with iPhone SE 2020.

Firstly, activate the keyboard by turning it on, then on your iPhone SE 2020, move to Settings, then to Bluetooth. Here, you will enable the Bluetooth, search for available devices and tap on the keyboard when it shows up on the list.

As soon as it is paired, the keyboard connects automatically to the iPhone any time the iPhone is in range (estimated to be about 10 meters), and the iPhone's Bluetooth is enabled. During the period of using the wireless keyboard, the iPhone's onscreen keyboard doesn't come up.

To switch off the wireless keyboard when it is not being used, simply press and delay your touch on the power switch until the green light on the wireless keyboard goes off.

Bluetooth Gadgets

Bluetooth gadgets can be used with the iPhone SE 2020, these gadgets include wireless headphones, car kits, speakers, and many others. However, several accessories have certain effects on the strength of wireless connections when they are connected to the iPhone SE 2020. Not all accessories meant for iPod or iPad are compatible with the iPhone. Furthermore, when airplane mode is enabled, it may interrupt the connection between the iPhone and an accessory that is linked to it. Changing the orientation or the position of both the iPhone and the accessory connected may have a positive effect on the performance of the wireless connection.

Enabling or Disabling the Bluetooth

The Control Center is a quick path to enable or disable the Bluetooth. Simply pull it up and tap on the Bluetooth icon to enable to disable the function.

Getting Your Phone Paired with a Bluetooth Device

Follow the laid down guidelines that came with the device when putting the device in discovery mode to facilitate its connection. On your iPhone SE 2020, move to Settings, then to Bluetooth. Here, you will enable Bluetooth, search for available devices and tap on the device you want to connect with when it shows up on the list.

Perhaps you are also in possession of AirPods and you set the AirPods up with an iOS device or Mac computer. The AirPods set up will automatically connect on your other Apple devices the moment you log in with the same iCloud account used on the original set up device.

Switching Audio when Connected to a Bluetooth Device

When you're listening to music and you are also connected to a Bluetooth device, drag down from the crest edge of the screen to display the lock screen or wake the iPhone SE 2020. Then tap the output audio icon and pick your desired audio output.

Moreover, output changes back to iPhone by itself when the Bluetooth gadget is no longer within range.

To use the iPhone speaker or receiver instead of the Bluetooth speaker to receive phone calls, tap on the iPhone's screen, or while you are receiving the call, tap on Audio and select iPhone or phone speaker option. A more effective way to do this is to simply turn off your Bluetooth gadget or move out of the gadget's range so it gets unpaired.

To remove a device from your Bluetooth paired list, select Forget This Device in the Bluetooth settings. In the case of AirPods, when you tap Forget This Device to remove the AirPods from your pair list, it is automatically erased from other devices that are linked to your iCloud account.

Wireless Charging Devices

The iPhone SE 2020 supports wireless charging and you can choose to charge your iPhone's battery by placing the iPhone SE 2020 upright on a Qi Wireless charger.

Chapter Twelve

Handoff

The Handoff feature enables you to keep on working on one Apple device at the point where you stopped on another. A significant number of applications on the iPhone and even some outsider applications support Handoff. A requirement to using the Handoff feature is to sign in to your iCloud account with the same Apple ID across all your devices. However, each of the devices must have its Bluetooth option enabled and in a range of no more than ten meters from each other.

Using Handoff to Switch Between Devices

The Handoff icon of the application you're utilizing on your Mac device will be displayed on the iPhone at the bottom edge of the iPhone's lock screen. You can drag up the screen to proceed on your iPhone with whatever it is that you are doing on the app on your Mac. If on the other hand, you intend to transfer from an iPhone to a Mac device, the Handoff icon of the application will be displayed on your Mac device at one end of the dock. You can click the icon to keep on working on the application.

Disabling Handoff on Your Device.

In the settings page of your iPhone, tap on General, then select Handoff.

Universal Clipboard

To enable this feature, you must ensure that you have signed into your iCloud on all the devices with the same details. Furthermore, your device must have an active Wi-Fi network that it is connected to. These devices must also have their Bluetooth enabled and have to be within a range of 10 meters from one another and have Handoff activated on them. Universal clipboard enables you to copy contents, items on your iPhone SE 2020 and then paste it on another gadget with iOS software. The process of cutting, copying, and pasting these items has to be within a short timeframe.

Wi-Fi Calling on other Devices

Wi-Fi calling permits you to make and answer calls on your other Apple devices (iPad, iPod, or Mac) by transferring calls via your iPhone which must be active and linked to a cellular network. To make calls through this method, ensure that you have signed in to your iCloud account and FaceTime across all your devices using similar Apple ID details, also these devices need to be associated with the same active Wi-Fi network.

For easy setup, you should set up your iPhone first, then your other devices. However, logging out of either iCloud or FaceTime on your iPhone will lead to the Wi-Fi call being terminated.

Enabling Wi-Fi Calling on your iPhone SE 2020

Visit Settings on your iPhone, then tap on the Phone toggle. Proceed to select Wi-Fi Calling - this is where you enable the feature. In the instance that you come across Add Wi-Fi Calling for Other Devices, activate it to permit calls to come in from other devices. It is essential that your iPhone is powered on and associated with the same Wi-Fi network as other devices.

Enabling Wi-Fi Calling on your other devices (iPad or iPod touch).

On that device, go to Settings, then proceed to FaceTime and enable it. If asked, enable Wi-Fi calling.

A significant point to note here is that even though you have activated Wi-Fi calling, emergency calls always have a preference over Wi-Fi, therefore, information about the location of your device may be useful for emergency services to hasten response efforts, irrespective of whether your location services is enabled or not. Certain network carriers may go further to make use of the address you inputted as your location while registering with the network carrier while signing up for Wi-Fi calling.

Making a Call on Your Other Devices

To put a call through by using the iPad or iPod touch, simply tap on the intended phone number. Receiving a call on such devices requires you to pull up the notification panel and choose whichever call reception option you want.

Chapter Thirteen

Personal Hotspot

Personal Hotspot comes into play whenever you intend to share your iPhone's internet connection access. Computers can benefit from this feature via Wi-Fi linkage, Bluetooth, or by utilizing a USB cable. For other devices, they can only benefit from this internet sharing option via Wi-Fi. However, this mode of data sharing becomes effective only if the iPhone itself has an active connection to the Internet via the cellular data network.

Sharing an Internet Connection

To initiate the procedure of sharing the connection, go to Settings, then select "Cellular", and proceed to tap on the Personal Hotspot toggle. This makes room for the connection with your carrier. If your Personal Hotspot is enabled, you can associate with other devices through the following ways:

Wi-Fi (Wireless Fidelity)

On the device that you intend to share a connection with, enable the Wi-Fi and select your iPhone from the list of available Wi-Fi connection options.

USB

When the connection involves a computer, an extra option you can use to connect is via a USB cable. Once the connection has been made, check your computer's network preferences and select "iPhone", then set up the network arrangements.

Bluetooth

With your iPhone's Bluetooth enabled, pair and create a link with the Bluetooth device.

As soon as a device is connected to the iPhone, a blue band is displayed at the crest of the iPhone's screen. Also, the tag or name that your Personal Hotspot bears changes when you change the name of your iPhone. You can change your password anytime and as often as you want in the Hotspot section in Settings. You can also view and observe your cellular data usage by tapping on the cellular toggle in settings.

Transfer Files using iTunes

To enable this, associate your iPhone with your computer by means of the included USB cable, then on the iTunes application on your computer, pick "iPhone" and proceed to click Applications. Exchanging items between the iPhone and your computer is done using the File Sharing section.

Applications that are compatible with file sharing are displayed in the file-sharing Application list present in iTunes. To erase an item, select the file in the Documents list on your computer, at that point, press the delete key.

Chapter Fourteen

CarPlay

This feature allows applications on the iPhone to be present on your car's innate display. CarPlay provides a lot of benefits such as access to turnabout directions, conversing via calls and texts, listening to music, and much more. However, CarPlay is only accessible on certain automobiles, areas and navigation systems. Moreover, Siri must be activated on your iPhone.

CarPlay is controlled via your car's programmed controls such as the touch screen or touchpad. You can use the Siri Voice command to instruct CarPlay on whatever it is that you want without making any physical contact with your iPhone. You can instruct Siri to make a call, tune in to a song, converse with a text message, discover directions, check your notifications, set a reminder, and lots more.

Get Started

If your vehicle bolsters remote CarPlay, press and hold the voice order button on the steering wheel to begin CarPlay setup. To connect your iPhone to your vehicle's USB port, utilize an Apple-affirmed Lightning to USB cable. It might be marked with the CarPlay logo, the word CarPlay, or a picture of a cell phone. Depending on the model of your vehicle, the CarPlay Home screen may show up consequently.

Associate Wirelessly to CarPlay

To start with, ensure your vehicle is compatible with remote or wireless CarPlay and is in remote or Bluetooth pairing mode. From there, go to Settings > General > CarPlay > Available Cars, and pick your vehicle.

Address Siri

Press and hold the voice order button on the steering wheel or touch and hold the Home button on the CarPlay home screen, until Siri signals. At that point tell Siri your request. You can also let go of the button to let Siri know when you are done talking.

Open an Application

Tap the application on the touch screen, or bend the revolving knob to choose the application, pushing down when you reach the application you want to open.

Come Back to the CarPlay Home Screen

You can press the "back" button close to the turning knob or press and hold the "back" button until you return to the Home screen.

Return to the Vehicle Home Screen

Press the manual home button on your iPhone or the vehicle's logo if it is displayed on the home screen.

View Extra Applications

When the number of applications is more than eight, some applications may show up on another page of the Home screen. Swipe left on the touchscreen or turn the rotating knob.

Come Back to a Recently Utilized Application

Tap its symbol on the edge of the touchscreen, or wind the rotary knob to the symbol, pushing down on the knob at the right point.

Scroll Rapidly Through a List

Tap the letters along the rundown on the right side of the touch screen or bend the rotational handle.

View and Control the Present Sound Source

Tap on Now Playing to have a look at the current sound application.

Rework the Symbols on the CarPlay Home

Go to Settings, select General, then tap on CarPlay on your iPhone. Select your vehicle. Touch and hold an icon. To remove an icon, tap it. To include it again, tap it once more (an icon that can be removed shows up with a dim hover in its upper-left corner). Your symbol changes show up on the CarPlay Home screen whenever you connect with CarPlay.

Chapter Fifteen

Siri and Maps

Use Siri or launch Maps to get directions, traffic updates, and estimated travel time. CarPlay creates predicted destinations using addresses from your email, instant messages, contacts, and schedules, as well as spots you visit often. You can scan for an area, use areas you bookmarked, and find close by attractions and places of interest.

You can utilize different applications in any event, while getting bearings. CarPlay tells you at the point when it's a great opportunity to make a turn.

You can enquire with Siri by stating sentences like, 'Take me to the office', or, 'Provide me with directions to the nearest viewing center.'

Show Probable Destination

Open Maps, then select Destinations. Pick a destination in the rundown to get headings. To get headings to a close-by service, select a category, (for example, Gas or Coffee), then select a place.

Make a fast temporary reroute.

To make a stop while exploring in Maps, select the search tool, then select one of the recommended services (for example, Gas Stations), at that point select a destination to your route.

Chapter Sixteen

Privacy and Security On iPhone SE 2020

The iPhone SE 2020 in line with the tradition of Apple values the privacy of her users, however this privacy can be further enhanced through various other features that the phone offers.

Location Services

Location Services permits area-based applications, for example, Reminders, Maps, Camera, and Wallet to accumulate and use information showing your area. Your estimated location is resolved by utilizing accessible information from cellular setup data, neighborhood Wi-Fi systems (if you have Wi-Fi turned on), and GPS (if accessible). When an application is using Location Services, a slanting arrow is displayed in the status bar.

Privacy preferences enable you to observe and control which applications and framework services can access information about Location Services, and Contacts, Calendars, Reminders, and Photographs.

Enacting or Disabling Location Services

Go to Settings on your iPhone, then Privacy and tap on Location Services. You can disable the feature for a few or for all applications and services.

Disabling Location Services off for System services.

A few framework services, for example, compass alignment and area-based advertisements, use Location Services. To view their status, enable or disable them, go to Settings > Privacy, move to Location Services, then click on System Services.

Restrict Access to Private Information.

Go to Settings > Privacy. Here, you will get to know which applications and features have access to private data with your permission. You can disable each applications permission to each one of these classifications of data:

- Contacts
- Schedules
- Updates/Reminders
- Photographs
- Bluetooth Sharing
- Mouthpiece/Microphone
- Speech Recognition
- Camera
- Health
- Home Kit
- Media and Apple Music
- Movement and Fitness

Audit the terms and privacy approach for every outsider application to understand how it uses the information it requires.

Advertising and Following

Disable area-based promotions and offers.

Go to Settings > Privacy > Area Services > System Services. At that point, turn off Location-Based Apple Promotions.

Reset or Regulate Ad Tracking.

Go to Settings, select Privacy, proceed to Advertising (at the base of the screen). To clear your data, tap Reset Advertising Identifier. To quit intended promotions, enable Limit Ad Tracking.

Accessing the information Apple uses to convey targeted promotions.

Go to Settings on your iPhone, then select Privacy, proceed to Advertising, then pick View Ad information. This data is used by Apple to decide on promotions shown in Apple News and the App Store. Your exclusive data isn't made available for outsider parties.

Restrict Your Safari Browsing logs to Yourself.

While browsing the web, you can restrict cross-site trailing, block threats, delete your perusing history, and so on. For more enlightenment, go to Settings > Privacy > Advertising > About Advertising and Privacy.

Security

Utilize a password with data security

For enhanced security, you can put in place a password that must be entered each time you turn on or wake up your iPhone.

Setting and Altering the password

Go to Settings, select Touch ID and Password. To change when your iPhone automatically locks and requires the password to open, go to Settings > Display and Brightness > Auto-Lock.

Putting a password in place enhances security. Use your password as a key to encode Mail messages and connections saved on iPhone, utilizing 256-piece AES encryption. (Different applications may likewise utilize information protection.)

Include fingerprints and set alternatives for the Touch ID sensor

Go to Settings on your iPhone, then to Touch ID, then Passcode.

Permit access to Features when iPhone SE 2020 is Locked

Go to Settings, proceed to Touch ID and Passcode. Discretionary features include: Control Center, latest notifications, today view, respond with message, wallet, respond to missed calls, and home control.

Erase Data after 10 Failed Password Attempts

Go to Settings, then to Touch ID and Password, then tap Erase Data. After ten failed password attempts, all preferences are reset, all your data and media are deleted, and you should re-establish your gadget from a backup or set it up again from scratch.

Use two-factor Authentication for Securing your iPhone SE 2020

Two-factor validation is an additional piece of security for your Apple ID, intended to guarantee that you're the only person who can get into your account, regardless whether somebody knows your secret code.

Enabling Two-factor Validation

Switch it on when asked while setting up your iPhone, or go to Settings > [your name], then select Password and Security. At that point, tap Turn on Two-Factor Authentication.

When requested, confirm your identity with a six-digit check code (as depicted below). You won't be requested to provide a check code again on your iPhone except if you sign out totally, eradicate your iPhone, sign in to your Apple ID account site in

Safari on your iPhone, or need to change your Apple ID secret key for security reasons.

Authenticating your Identity

When enquiring on your iPhone for the code, search for a notification on any of your trusted gadgets or at a trusted telephone number. On a trusted gadget, tap Allow to cause a code to show up on that gadget. To send the code to a trusted telephone number, tap "Didn't get a confirmation code?", then select the phone number and enter the code sent to your iPhone.

If you can't get a confirmation code on your trusted gadgets, and a trusted telephone number is inaccessible, you can get a confirmation code from Settings whether your gadget is disconnected from an internet connection or not. On a trusted iOS gadget, go to Settings > [your name], proceed to Password and Security, at that point tap Get Verification Code.

Include Another iOS Gadget as Confided-in Gadget

After enabling two-factor authentication, utilize the same Apple ID to sign in to iCloud on another gadget. Confirm your identity with a six-digit check code (as depicted previously). You can get confirmation codes on the entirety of your trusted gadgets.

Include a Trusted Telephone Number

Go to Settings > [your name], then to Password and Security, proceed to tap Edit (above the rundown of trusted telephone numbers), at that point tap Add a trusted Phone Number.

You should confirm at least one trusted telephone number to partake in two-factor authentication. You should consider confirming other telephone numbers you can get to, for example, a home telephone, or a number utilized by a relative or companion. Trusted telephone numbers don't consequently get verification codes. In the event that you can't procure an entry to any trusted gadgets when setting up another gadget for two-factor validation, tap "Didn't get a confirmation code?" on the new gadget, then pick one of your trusted telephone numbers to get the confirmation code.

Expel a Trusted Telephone Number

Go to Settings > [your name], then to Password and Security, proceed to tap Edit (over the rundown of saved telephone numbers), at that point, tap the red symbol close to the telephone number.

To disable two-factor authentication, you have to sign in to your Apple ID account, proceed to select Security, then tap Edit. At this point, tap Turn Off Two-Factor Authentication.

Setting Up Your Touch ID for Various Functions on the iPhone SE 2020

You can open the iPhone by simply placing a registered finger on the Home button. Touch ID also permits you to:

Utilize your Apple ID secret code to make purchases in the iTunes Store, App Store, or iBooks Store.

Approve payments for items purchased through Apple Pay.

Make information pertaining to debit or credit cards available to you.

Charging and transporting addresses, and contact data while making payments in an application that supports Apple Pay as a strategy for payment.

Utilize different features in some outsider apps.

Set up the Touch ID Sensor

Go to Settings > Touch ID and Passcode. Set your preference of using a fingerprint to open the iPhone, and to settle expenses. Select Add a Fingerprint, then follow the on-screen guidelines. You can include different fingerprints (both of your thumbs and index fingers, and even one for your companion).

Note: If you switch off your iPhone after setting up the Touch ID, you will be asked to input your password upon turning it back on. You'll also need your Apple ID secret code for any purchase you make in the iTunes Store, App Store, or iBooks Store.

Erase a Fingerprint

Select the fingerprint, then tap Delete Fingerprint. If you have more than one fingerprint, position a finger on the Home button to discover which one it is.

Tag a Fingerprint

Select the fingerprint you want to name, then enter the name of your choice.

Utilize the Touch ID sensor to make a payment on the iTunes Store, AppStore, or Books Store.

When buying from the iTunes Store, or any store on the iPhone SE 2020, follow the guidelines to make purchases with your fingerprint. You can also go to Settings > Touch ID and Passcode, then enable iTunes and App Store.

Use Touch ID for Apple Pay

Go to Settings on your iPhone SE 2020, select Touch ID and Passcode to guarantee that Apple Pay is enabled with Touch ID.

Chapter Seventeen

Make a call

Putting a call through on the iPhone SE 2020 is simple, it is simply by selecting a number from your contacts, tapping one of your favorites or a number from the previous call log.

Using Siri or Voice Control to Make Calls

Firstly, you activate Siri, then say "call" or "dial" a name or number which you will pronounce. You can include a unique catchphrase to specify the contact you intend to reach such as at home, at school, and so on. When voice dialing a number, pronounce every digit independently for instance, "four, six, five..."

Add Favorite Contacts

With Favorites, you can make a call with a single tap. To include a contact to your Favorites list, tap the add icon. You can also add names to Favorites from Contacts. In the Contacts application, select "Add to Favorites" at the base of the contact's card, then proceed to select the number, and the contact will be added to your favorite list. To delete a name or adjust your Favorites list, tap Edit.

Returning a Recent Call

Tap the Recent tab in your Contacts app, then Tap call. In case you want to obtain access to more information about the call, or the contact who made the call, tap the information icon, and that does it. A red tag serves as an indicator of the number of missed calls.

Dial a Call

In the contacts app, tap the keypad, then input the number, then tap the call button. Alternatively, if the number is saved on your phone, select the number in the Contacts app, then tap the call button.

Inputting a Number to the Keypad:

Swiftly double-tap the phone number box just above the keypad, then tap Paste.

-Enter a delicate (2-second) delay: Tap the asterisk key for a few seconds until a comma shows up.

-Bring in a hard pause (to put a halt to dialing until you tap the Dial button): Place your touch on the "#" key until a semicolon is displayed.

-Input a "+" for universal calls: Tap the zero (0) key for a few seconds until "+" is displayed.

-Redial the immediately previous number: Tap Keypad, then proceed to tap "Call" to bring up the number, then tap the call icon.

Receiving a Call on Your iPhone SE 2020

Select or swipe to Accept to pick an incoming call. Or then again, if the iPhone is locked, Tap the Home button. You can also Tap the center button on your EarPods to receive calls and execute other actions just as it had been stated earlier.

Silencing an Incoming Call.

To execute this, tap any of the side buttons on your iPhone, this includes either of the two-volume buttons. The option of answering the call, even after you've silenced it, is still very much opened to you till the moment it goes into voicemail. Moreover, you can reset your iPhone to announce incoming calls and indicate the situations in which the feature should come into play when you're using earphones, to implement this, go to Setting, select Phone, then tap on Announce Calls.

Rejecting Calls and Utilizing Voicemail

There are numerous ways of doing this, they include:

- Taping the side button twice in rapid succession.
- Tap on the middle button on your headset for up to two seconds. Two faint beeps that will be heard affirm that the call was rejected.
- You can simply tap Decline

However, in certain zones, declined calls are disengaged without being sent to the voice recorder.

Sending Instant Messages as Replies

To activate this, tap Message, select an intended reaction, reply, or tap Custom. To make your default reactions, go to Settings, select Phone, then select Respond with Text, move further by selecting any of the default messages, and supplant it with your content.

Getting Prompts to Return Calls

To make use of this option, tap Remind Me and set when you want to be reminded.

Block Unwanted Callers

There are situations in which you'll receive calls from contacts that you don't want, to evade subsequent occurrences, select the "Block this Caller" on the contact's card. You can also block these contacts in Settings, go to Settings, select Phone, then tap Blocking and Identification. By implication, voice calls, FaceTime calls, or instant messages will not be gotten from these blocked guests.

Identify Spam Calls

Download a spam-blocking application, which will be of massive aid in executing this, from the App Store, and iPhone prompts you of hovering spam calls.

Multitasking When on a Call

While on a call, Tap the Home button which will take you to the home screen, then open the application. To revisit the call, tap the green bar which is displayed at the top of the screen.

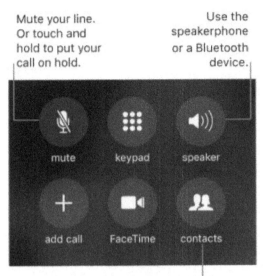

Mute your line. Or touch and hold to put your call on hold.

Use the speakerphone or a Bluetooth device.

mute   keypad   speaker

add call   FaceTime   contacts

Get contact info.

React to a Subsequent Calls

When it comes to this, you can choose to:

- Neglect the call and so it converted to a voicemail, or you tap Ignore.

- Pause the main call and answer the incoming one, to execute this, tap Hold + Accept

- End the present call and answer the new one.

If a GSM network is being used, tap End + Accept. On a CDMA network, you can tap End so that when the second call comes in, you can then tap on Accept, or if the phone is locked, you can drag the slider instead.

While a call is being held, tap Swap to flip between calls, or select Merge Calls to converse with the two contacts simultaneously without any interruption.

Setting Up a Conference Call

With GSM, you are entitled to set up a conference call with up to five individuals. Conference calls may not be accessible if your call is utilizing VoLTE (Voice over LTE) or Wi-Fi calling.

Initiating a Conference Call

While you are active on a call, tap Add Call, make another call, then tap Merge Calls. Repeat this process to add more individuals to the call.

Drop One Individual

Tap the information button close to an individual and tap End.

Talk Secretly with One Individual

To engage in a secret conversation with a member of the conference, tap the information button, then select Private close to the individual. When you are done with the conversation, tap Merge Calls to return to the conference call.

Include a New Caller

To include a new caller into the conference, tap Hold Call, then choose Answer, and, tap Merge Calls.

International Calls

For information about making worldwide calls from your home region (local rates and different charges may apply), contact your carrier.

When traveling abroad, you have the option to use your iPhone to make calls, converse via instant messages, receive visual or voice messages, and use applications, surf the Web and access other permissible network applications allowed in your new location.

Set Network Alternatives

Visit Settings, then tap Cellular. You will be provided with a list of options that include enabling or disabling voice or data roaming, enabling or disabling cellular data connection, using GSM network connection outside your region.

Disabling Cellular Services

Visit Settings on your iPhone, then enable Airplane Mode, tap Wi-Fi and turn it on. Calls coming in are directed to a voice recorder. To continue using cellular network services, disable Airplane Mode.

Emergency Calls

In case there's an emergency, you can rapidly make a call for help with the iPhone.

Make an Emergency from a Locked Screen

Tap the Emergency Call option displayed on your phone screen, input the emergency number, then dial it.

Enable Auto Call

Go to Settings, then proceed to Emergency SOS. If Auto Call has been enabled and you initiate an emergency SOS call, iPhone plays a cautioning sound and then commences a count down and puts a call through to the emergency unit in your area. The iPhone plays the countdown sound regardless of whether the iPhone is in silent mode or the Do Not Disturb feature has been enabled. To get rid of this sound, go to Settings > Emergency SOS.

Prompt your Emergency Contacts

After making an emergency SOS call, iPhone prompts your emergency contacts that you made a call and sends them your present location (if accessible).

Visual Voicemail

Visual voice messages provide you with a rundown of your messages. You can pick which ones you intend to listen to, see translations of messages, or delete them, without going through every one of them. A tag on the Voicemail icon informs you about the number of messages you haven't attended to. On your first experience with the Voicemail option, you're asked to set up a voice message secret code and record your voice messages greeting

Listen to a Voice Message

Tap Voicemail, then proceed to select a message, then tap the play icon. If a visual voice message isn't accessible with your service, tap Voicemail, then adhere to the voice instructions. Furthermore, Siri can also play a role here, you can say something like: "Play the voicemail from John", "How many new voicemails do I have?". Messages are stored until you delete them or until they're being removed by your carrier.

Delete a Message

To get rid of a certain voice message off your list, tap or swipe left on the message, then tap Delete. In certain zones, deleted messages might be forever deleted. Your voice messages may also be deleted if you change your SIM card.

Managing Deleted Messages

Display a rundown of the messages, then select Delete Messages. This enables you to:

- Listen to a deleted message by tapping the message.

- Restore a deleted message: This is done by tapping the message followed by tapping "Undelete".

- Delete a message permanently: Swipe left on the message and tap Clear.

To avoid the stress of erasing all the messages one after the other, you can delete all the messages once permanently by simply tapping "Clear All".

Share a Message

Other than the delete option, you are also enabled to share a message, this is executed when you tap on the message, followed by tapping on the Share icon.

Modify your Welcome Message

An earlier set voicemail welcome message or greeting can be modified. Tap Voicemail, select Greeting, tap Custom, then tap Record.

Set Alarm Sound for New Message

Users may intend to be notified whenever a new voicemail comes in, to activate this, go to Settings > Sounds.

Change the Voicemail Password

Just like in every other aspect of the iPhone SE2020, the password can also be changed here, to change your voicemail password, go to Settings > Phone > Change Voicemail password. In case you seem not to remember your voice message password, your wireless carrier is in the best position to help you out with that.

Managing Contacts

Tap the add button in the number you intend to add to your contact. iPhone automatically recommends new contacts from messages sent to you in Mail and invitations, events in Calendar, and from several applications. To disable this component, go to Settings, tap Contacts, then select Siri and

Search, then disable the "Find Contacts in Other Applications" component.

To permit incoming messages or calls from a contact regardless of whether Do Not Disturb is on. Tap the contact, select Edit, go on to Tap Ringtone, or Text Tone, then activate Emergency Bypass.

Finding Contacts

Tap the inquiry field at the top of the contacts list, then enter your inquiry. You can also look through your contacts utilizing the Search button.

To swiftly reach a contact in the app, tap one of the buttons under the contact's name to initiate a message, call, video call, or email. To change the default contact method (for a call, for instance), touch and hold the call button, then select a telephone number.

Perhaps you utilize an outsider or third-party application to carry out these activities (make calls, send messages, or converse via email), you might have the option to set that application as the default.

Change the Display Manner of your Contacts

Go to Settings, then select Contact, you can implement the changes here.

Share Contact

Select a contact, then tap "Share Contact." Sharing contacts gives you access to information from the contact's card.

Attach a Picture to a Contact

Select the contact you want to attach a photo, then tap Edit, all you need to do now is to include the picture by Taping "add a photo." This provides you with the option of either snapping a picture instantly with your camera or include one from the Photos application.

Change a Label

If a field has an inappropriate label, for example, Home rather than Work, tap Edit. Select a label from the rundown or tap Add Custom Label to make one of your own.

Include your Contacts' Social Profiles

While displaying a contact, while seeing a contact, tap Edit, then tap "add social profile."

Removing a Contact

Go to the contact's card, then tap Edit. Go through the list of options, then tap Delete Contact.

Include your Contact Information

iPhone utilizes your Apple ID to make your "My Card", yet you may need to fill in certain information by yourself to finish it.

Complete your "My Card."

Launch the Contacts app, then select My Card option which is displayed at the top of your contacts list, then tap Edit. Contacts addresses and telephone numbers to assist you with setting up your My Card. If there is no My Card, tap +, then enter your data. To make a My Card with this provided information, go to Settings > Contacts, tap My Info, then tap your name in the Contacts list.

Update your "My Card" Information

In the Contacts app, tap My Card at the top of your contacts list, then tap Edit.

Include Contact Accounts

Other than including contacts independently, you can:

-**Use your iCloud contacts:** Go to Settings, select [your name], select iCloud, then turn on Contacts.

-**Utilize your Google contacts:** Go to Settings, select Accounts, and Passwords. Tap Google, sign in to your registered account, then turn on Contacts.

-**Include contacts from another account:** Go to Settings, select Accounts and Passwords, then tap Add Account. Pick an account and sign into it, then turn on Contacts.

-**Access a Microsoft Exchange Global Address List:** Go to Settings, select Records and Passwords. Tap Exchange, sign in to your Exchange account, then turn on Contacts.

-Set up an LDAP and CardDAV record to get to business or school catalogs: Go to Settings, select Accounts, and Passwords, pick Add Account, then select Other. Tap Add LDAP record or Add CardDAV account, then enter the account data.

-Sync contacts from your PC: In iTunes on your PC, tap Info displayed in the device info sheet, then select Sync Contacts.

-Bring in contacts from a SIM card (GSM): With a new SIM card installed on the iPhone, go to Settings select Contacts, then tap Import SIM Contacts.

-Bring in contacts from a vCard: Select a .vcf attachment in an email or message.

Show or Conceal a Group

Tap on the Groups option and select the groups you desire to see. This button shows up just If you have more than one means of getting contacts.

Include a Favorite

Include important contacts in your Favorites list for snappy dialing. Select a Contact, and on that page, scroll down and select Add to Favorites. Calls from these contacts have an edge over the Do Not Disturb option.

Save a Number Recently Dialed

In the phone app, tap Keypad, enter a number, then tap the add icon. Proceed to tap Create New Contact, or select Add to Existing Contact, then pick a contact.

Remove Duplicate Contacts

At the point when you have contacts from different sources, you may have various entry format for an individual. To avoid repetitive contacts from showing up in your All Contacts list, contacts from various sources with a similar name are connected and shown as a solitary classified contact. At moments when you view unified contact, the title Unified Info shows up.

Link Contacts

When several inputs for a certain individual do not connect automatically, you can bring them together manually. Tap one of the contacts, select Edit, then Tap Link Contacts. Select the other contact entry to interface with and Tap Link.

At the point when you connect contacts with various first or other names, the names on each contact do not change, yet just one name shows up on the unified card. To select which name shows up on the unified card, tap one of the linked cards, then tap the contact's name on that card, and tap Use This Name for Unified Card. However, when you connect contacts, those contacts aren't combined. If you change or include data in a unified contact, the alterations are duplicated to each source account which has the data.

Call Forwarding

The call forwarding icon shows up in the status bar when the call sending is on. You should be within the scope of the cellular network when you set iPhone to forward calls, otherwise, calls will not be forwarded.

Call Waiting

In case you're on a call and call waiting has been disabled, new calls coming are instantly directed to voice mail.

Caller ID

For FaceTime calls, your telephone number is shown regardless of whether the caller ID is activated or not.

For CDMA accounts, be in touch with your carrier for data about enacting and utilizing these features.

Ringtones and Vibrations

Along with the iPhone comes ringtones that are sounded for incoming calls, set alarms, and the clock timer. You can also purchase ringtones from songs in the iTunes Store

Set the Default Ringtone

Go to Settings, select Sounds and Haptics, then choose Ringtone.

Assign an Alternate Ringtone to a Contact

Go to Contacts, select the contact you intend to assign a ringtone to. Tap Edit, band picks a ringtone.

Enabling or Disabling Vibration

As opposed to the iPhone ringing, vibration is an alternative to way be informed when there is an incoming call, to enable or disable the vibration component, go to Settings, select Sounds and Haptics.

Set the Ring Tone for New Messages

Although there is a default alert tone put in place for messages on the iPhone, you can set new alarm tones, to do this, go to Settings, select Sounds and Haptics, then choose New Voicemail.

Chapter Eighteen

Safari

Browse the web

With Safari on iPhone, you can surf the web, include additional pages to your reading list for later use, and attach page icons to the Home screen for speedy access. If you sign in to iCloud with the same Apple ID on all your Apple devices, the option of viewing pages you have opened on different devices, and keeping your bookmarks, history, and reading list, with them being up to date, will be made available to you on your other gadgets.

Block pop-ups. Go to Settings, select Safari, then Block Pop-up.

Website View Menu

The search field on safari is the component used to search or input URLs, on the left side of this search field, there is an icon denoted by "aA". Touching this aA icon leads you to the Website View menu, here, a list of options will be displayed:

Content Size option: Reset the size of the content particularly the text, on the site you're on.

-Enable reader view: Activates Reader on the site you're on at that moment, which disposes off advertisement, thereby setting up a perfect book-style reading interface.

-**Conceal Toolbar:** Takes out the Toolbar so you can see the site page you're on full screen.

- View the desktop rendition of a site displays the desktop version of a site instead of the mobile rendition. This transforms into "Request Mobile Website" if the desktop version of that webpage is already in use.

-**Website Settings:** This is where you configure all your setting for the websites you are able to visit from your iPhone. You can set the webpage you're active on in the browser to process contents by itself in reader view or to consistently process the contents in the desktop version. Also, you can enable or disable content blockers on every site, and switch access to the camera, mouthpiece, and your location. You can always access websites where you've modified the settings in the Safari section of the Settings application underneath "Website Settings."

Search the web

Enter a URL or search term in the search field positioned at the top of the page, based on the searched term, suggestions of what you intend to input will be provided, you can tap on any of these suggestions that suit your exact search, these suggestions help you to quickly search a site you've visited previously. Or you can decide not to select any suggestion hence, you utilize the keyboard to input your search. Perhaps you would prefer not to see these recommended search terms, go to Settings, select Safari, then disable Search Engine Suggestions

Search a Page

To locate a word or sentence in a Web page, tap the share icon, then select Find in Page. Input the word you intend to find in the search field to search. To choose a search engine, go to the Safari section in Settings.

Managing Bookmarks

While you are on that page, tap the bookmark icon at bottom of the page. To see another organizer, delete, rename, or reorder bookmarks, tap Edit.

Add a Website Page as Favorite

Open the webpage, tap the share icon, then tap Add to Favorites

Edit Favorites

In cases whereby you intend to rearrange, remove or rename certain entries in your favorites list, tap the bookmark icon, then tap the Bookmarks tab, proceed to select Favorites, then tap Edit to delete, rename, or reorder your favorites. Another option lets you select which favorite show up when you tap the search field on your browser, to enact this, go to Settings, select Safari, then choose Favorites.

Save a Reading List for Later

Save intriguing items in your reading list so you can return to them later. You can even store the content of your reading list to your iCloud and go through them later when there is no Internet connection.

Add the present page to your reading list

To include a page, you're active on to your reading list, tap the share icon, then select Add to Reading List. To include a linked page without visiting the page, touch and hold the page link, then tap Add to Reading List in the options.

View your Reading List

To display and view your reading list, tap the bookmark icon, then Tap the view button.

Remove an Item from Reading List

In a bid to edit your reading list, you can delete certain items from your reading list by swiping them to the left side of the screen.

Store Items Automatically on Reading List to iCloud for Offline Usage

Offline reading of items on your reading list is made easy by being automatically saved on your iCloud account. To enable this, go to Settings, select Safari, then enable Automatically Save Offline.

Fill in Forms

During moments of signing into a site, signing up for a site, or making an online purchase, you can fill in the information required in Web form, with the use of the onscreen keyboard, or have Safari assist you through AutoFill. To enable or disable AutoFill, go to Settings, select Safari, tap AutoFill, then select either option.

AutoFill also saves you the time of always inputting your details whenever you want to log in to a site. To have it enabled, when asked if you want to save your password for the site, tap Yes. Whenever you visit, your username and password are filled in for you.

Sign in with an Alternate Identity

If you have registered with a certain site using several identities, and an erroneous identity is filled in, tap Passwords above the keyboard, then select the personality you prefer.

Include a Credit Card for Purchases

To make online purchases faster and without the monotony of having to input your card details every time you initiate a transaction, it is important that you add your credit card, to do this, go to Settings, select Safari, choose AutoFill, proceed to tap on Saved Credit Cards, then Add Credit Card. To enter the card details without typing, tap Use Camera, then position iPhone so that your card shows up in the frame. Also, when you make an online purchase, you can permit Safari to retain the credit card details.

Utilize Reader for Interruption-free Reading

Safari interruption-free reading enables you to go through a page devoid of advertisements, redirections, or other distracting content. To enable this, Tap the aA icon which is displayed at the top left-hand side of the search bar, then select Show Reader View. Also, a quicker method to activate the reader's view is to Tap on the Aa icon until the readers' view is displayed.

Privacy and Security

By changing a few of the Safari settings, you can increase your chances of being able to keep your browsing activities private and shield yourself from harmful websites. To control privacy and security settings for Safari, go to Settings, select Safari, tap on "Privacy and Security." Here, you can:

Forestall Cross-site Tracking:

Safari restricts outsider cookies and information by default. Disabling this component implies that cross-site tracking will be permitted.

-Block cookies from every entry: To evacuate cookies that have already found their way into the iPhone, go to Settings >Safari, choose Clear History and Website Data.

-Ask sites not to trail you: However, certain websites can decide not to heed to request therefore beware!

-Get cautious about phony websites: Safari shows an admonition in case you're visiting a suspected phishing site.

View your Saved Passwords

All the passwords you have ever made use of and saved on safari are stored and can be displayed if you know how to make that happen. To access them, go to Settings, select "Records and Passwords," then tap on "App and Site Passwords," next, input your iPhone password or use Touch ID. This is very useful when your device has been made to remember all your passwords, but you are trying to log in on another device of PC and can no longer remember your password, you can use this option to remember your password.

Delete your Browsing History and Data

To clear records of your browsing activities, go to Settings, select Safari, tap on Clear History and Website Data.

Visit Sites Without Recording History

The private mode on safari is what allows you to browse privately and securely without the history being added to the history page in safari. To activate this, tap the minimize screen icon and select Private. To conceal these sites and leave private browsing mode, also, tap the minimize screen icon, then tap

Private. However, these sites will come up later when you make use of the Private browsing mode unless you clear the page.

Chapter Nineteen

Managing Messages

Send and Get Messages

With the Messages application, you can converse through texting, sending pictures, videos. You can also send additional content through iMessage or with the aid of SMS/MMS services. Furthermore, iMessage provides you with the extra features of allowing you enhance your messages with bubble impacts, undetectable ink, full-screen impacts, your penmanship, Computerized or digital touch, iMessage applications, animoji and memoji stickers, and other features.

Start a Discussion

To initiate a discussion on Messages, tap the compose icon, proceed to input the beneficiary's telephone number or email address, or on the other hand, if the recipient is a saved contact on your iPhone, tap + and select that contact. When in the contact page, to start typing, touch the text box, then type in your message and when you're done typing, tap the upward directional arrow to send the message.

Manage a Group Discussion

In a group, tap the info icon to display a list of options of what you can do on the group. You can give the discussion a tag, include somebody to the discussion, or leave the discussion.

React with a Tap back

To send a quick response that tells individuals what you're thinking, tap the message you want to react to, then select your response.

View and Oversee Discussion Subtleties

To view the details about a conversation, tap the info icon and this allows you to:

- Have a glance at the contact card of selected contacts.

- Execute speedy actions, for example, making a call.

- Send your present location or make your location available for sharing for a predefined length of time.

- Shroud Alerts.

- Dispatch read receipts.

- Display pictures and attachments.

Display the Message list

To have a full view of the Messages list, tap <, or slide the screen from the left edge.

Search Discussions

Swipe the Messages list to the top to uncover the search field, next, type in the content you're searching for. You can as well search for discussions from the Home screen.

Delete a Discussion

To delete a conversation, you've had with a contact or group when you're in the Messages list, swipe left on the discussion, and tap Delete. However, deleted conversations cannot be retrieved.

Set up iMessage and SMS/MMS

An Apple service that transmits messages over Wi-Fi or cellular remote connections with different iOS gadgets is the iMessage. Messages here do not in any way affect the normal messaging plan. Messages transmitted through iMessage can incorporate photographs, videos, as well as other information. You can see when others are composing messages and show proof that you have read messages sent by them. For security, conversations made through iMessage are encoded before they're transmitted. iMessage writings are exhibited in blue bubbles, meanwhile, SMS/MMS writings are displayed in green bubbles.

Sign in to iMessage

To gain access into your iMessage account by signing in, go to Settings, select Messages, and enable iMessage. In case you're signed in to iMessage with the exact Apple ID you've always utilized on the entirety of your devices, all the messages that you send and get on iPhone can also show up on your other Apple gadgets. Transmit a message from whichever gadget is nearest to you or make use of the handoff component to begin a discussion on one device and proceed with it on another device.

Send a Picture or Video

To send any form of media file when using iMessage, tap the camera icon in the conversation page, this provides you with a variety of options from which you can decide to:

-Select a picture or video from your photo library.

-Immediately snap a picture or video

-Make a selection from recent photos or videos by swiping to the left side of the screen in the contacts page on iMessage

-Snap a picture within Messages by framing the shot in the viewfinder and snap.

Whichever method of uploading media you've chosen, tap the upward directional arrow to send the media or tap the cancel button to eliminate the action.

Markup a Picture

Touch a picture in the message bubble, then tap Mark-up.

Send an Audio Message

To transmit an audio message, Tap and hold the microphone icon to record a message in the audio format, then release your touch on the icon to end the recording. After the recording process if you intend to listen to your audio message just before sending the audio message, tap the play button.

However, in a bid to conserve space on your iPhone, iPhone automatically deletes audio messages unless you've disabled that action in settings. To retain them, go to Settings, select Messages, then tap on Expire (below Audio Messages), then Tap Never.

Listening or Answering an Audio Message

Among the features of the iPhone is playing audio messages by simply raising the iPhone to your ear level, then you give a response to the message. To enable this component, or on the other hand, disable it, go to Settings, select Messages, then tap on the Raise to Listen option.

Forward a Message or Link

Touch and hold your touch on the message or attachment that you intend to forward, tap More and a rundown of options will be displayed, select extra items to forward if need be, then tap the Forward icon.

Sharing, Saving, or Printing an Attachment

The share icon lets you perform these functions on sent attachments when you tap and hold on them.

Duplicate an Attachment

To create a replica of an attachment, hold on the attachment, and select Copy in the list of options provided.

Delete a Message or Connection

To clear off a message or an attachment on Messages, hold your touch on that item and tap More to provide you with more options, select extra items if you want to, then tap the trash icon.

iMessage Applications

The iMessage applications offer you different methods with which you can improve a discussion with stickers, share items and so much more without the need to exit the Messages app. Increase your alternatives by downloading additional iMessage applications from the Application Store.

Browse and download iMessage applications

Adding more iMessage applications requires you to download them from the Applications Store, to do this, tap on the Apps Store icon.

Utilize iMessage Application

After downloading the iMessage app, tap the application to open it. If you want to bring in an item from the app into a conversation, tap the item thing. You can include a remark if you need to, then tap the upward directional arrow to send or tap × to cancel.

Enhance with Stickers

You are provided with a variety of stickers on the iMessage app, these stickers are the emoji, animoji, and emoji stickers. To attach a sticker to a message, tap on the sticker's application, which will also be displayed on your message screen. Touch and hold a sticker, then drag it to any message in the discussion. Before you discharge the sticker so it gets attached to a message, you can:

- Adjust the edge of the sticker: Turn a second finger around the finger hauling the sticker.

- Change the size of the sticker: Move another finger nearer to or away from the finger hauling the sticker.

These stickers can be attached to a message bubble, placed on another sticker, or then again even to spruce up a photograph. To uncover a text that is covered by a sticker.

View Sticker Subtleties

Make a touch contact and hold a sticker, then tap Sticker Details, this enables you to:

- View the sender of the sticker

- View the iMessage application from which the sticker was sent

- Delete the sticker by swiping left, then you get a list of options, tap Delete

Design Your Emoji's

You can come up with your personalized memojis. That is, you get to make your own choices of skin color, hairstyle, hair color, headwear, etc. You can design several memojis for several moods.

To design a memoji, tap the memoji icon in your conversation, then tap the add icon. Tap each feature and in each feature, make your selections. When you keep on making your selection in each feature, your memoji character comes to life. Tap Done to include the memoji to your stickers collection. To make any changes, copy or delete a memoji, tap on the memoji icon and tap the More button.

Manage iMessage Applications

To alter certain settings on the iMessage application, tap the More button, then tap Edit. You can:

-Drag the three horizontal lines to reorder applications.

-Tap the add icon to include an application to your favorites.

-Tap the remove icon to expel an application from your favorites.

-Disable the app to hide it.

Here are some applications that are automatically situated in the app drawer on iMessage.

Applications Store: you to download iMessage apps that you will utilize with Messages.

Photos: provides you with an avenue to include pictures into your conversation right from the application.

Digital Touch: Enables you to send taps, heartbeats, sketches, kisses, etc.

Music: With this, you can share songs you've just listened to from Apple Music.

Apple Pay: Transfer and receive money by making use of Apple pay.

#images: obtain access to numerous GIFs to include in your message.

Animoji: Design and share animated figures that make use of your voice and replicate your facial expressions.

Memoji: Design your personalized memoji stickers that suit your mood and attitude.

Remove an iMessage Application

To clear off an item from the iMessage application, tap the More button and swipe left on the iMessage application, then Tap Delete.

Digital Touch

With iMessage, you can utilize Computerized Contact to send taps, kisses, pulses, and many more. You can as well add this touch impact to a picture or video.

To create a Sketch, tap the digital touch icon, then draw with one finger. You can change the hue and then begin drawing once more. Tap the upward directional arrow to send.

Handwritten Messages

Another feature the iMessage application offers you is to send a message with your penmanship. The receiver views the animated form of the message just as ink is displayed on paper. While in the landscape, tap the text field and select the handwriting icon, then start to write with your finger. After typing, type Done and tap on the upward directional arrow to send or × to cancel it.

Animate Messages

Animation of messages and emojis are also possible with a single message with a bubble effect of fill the entire message screen with a full-screen effect. You can also send animated emojis by tapping on the emoji and holding the record button to input your voice and facial expressions.

Manage Message Notifications and Privacy

To alter notification settings, go to Settings, select Notifications, then tap on messages.

Set an Alert Sound for Messages

In the settings page on your iPhone, select Sound and Haptics, then tap on Text Tone.

Block Unwanted Messages and Calls

If you want to block conversations from a contact, tap on the conversation and select the info icon, proceed to view the contact card, then scroll down through the rundown and select Block this Caller. To view your list of blocked phone numbers and contact, go to Settings, select messages, and tap on Blocked.

Filter Messages from Strangers

Filtering iMessage messages disables notifications from senders whom you haven't saved their numbers on your iPhone and hence moves the messages to the Unknown Senders tab in the Messages list.

Chapter Twenty

Using the Music App

The music application on the iPhone allows you to enjoy the songs you have on your iPhone and also, music streamed over the Internet. Also, you can tune in to Beats 1 radio, which broadcasts throughout the day consistently from studios in Los Angeles, New York, and London. With a discretionary Apple Music membership, you are provided with a limitless amount of songs suggested by music specialists, to listen to and find new music along with your companions. An active Wi-Fi connection or cellular data connection is required to stream Apple Music and Radio, sometimes, an Apple ID is also required.

Access Music

Being an Apple Music member: Registering for a membership with Apple Music and having an active means of Internet connection, you are permitted to stream as much music as you like from the Apple Music index. You are also enabled to share playlists, collections, and stations with your companions, access and watch a vast number of movies, download songs, music albums, and even playlists.

Tune in to Beats 1: Beats 1 is an international radio station broadcasting live on Apple Music. Registration or enrolment for any form of membership isn't among the criteria to listen to Beats 1.

Use iCloud Music Library: Accessible to those who are registered as Apple Music members, iCloud music library entails all your imported and purchased music, alongside songs you included and downloaded from Apple Music. You can tune in to your music on any of your gadgets.

Take part in Family Sharing: Obtain an Apple Music Family Membership, and everyone present in your Family Sharing group can get the best out of Apple Music.

-Using iTunes to synchronize your music on your computer.

-Buy music from the iTunes Store on your iPhone.

Apple Music

Apple Music is best termed as a streaming music service that provides you with access to countless songs and your music library. As a member, you listen to songs at any time that suits you and in any mode of your choice either online or offline, you also get to select your playlist, recent music, ad-restricted radio, make choices pertaining movies and shows, songs played and shared by your pals and so much more.

Join Apple Music

Registering to join Apple Music can be done when you open the Music app, or in Settings > Music > Join Apple Music.

-**Individual membership:** grants you access to the entire Apple Music inventory, top recommendations, and on-demand radio broadcasts.

-**Family membership**: About six individuals can be entertained by boundless access to Apple Music on their gadgets.

-**Student membership:** obtain complete access to Apple Music, with customized suggestions, the best new music, and a cost intended for students.

In case you're a student at a qualifying school, you can register to join Apple Music for a limited participation cost for as long as four years (4 years). The time doesn't necessarily have to be limited, student memberships aren't accessible in all regions. If your Apple Music membership comes to an end, you cannot stream anymore on Apple Music songs, the choice you will be left with is to play Apple Music songs you downloaded.

Get Customized Recommendations

Apple Music learns the music you like and suggests tunes, collections, and playlists depending on your preferences.

Select your Preferred Genres and Artists

At the point when you first tap the "For You" option, you're demanded to give Apple some information about what you like and prefer. Select the genres you like by double-tapping them and for the genres that you have no listening passion for, tap, and hold on them so they will be removed. Tap Next and repeat the same process with the artists that show up.

To include an artist whom, you can't find in the list, tap Add an Artist, then enter the artist's name. Apple Music utilizes these inclinations while prescribing music to you.

Restrict Suggestions on Shared Gadgets

What you listen to on the Music app impacts on a feature on the iPhone known as "For You" suggestions. If you share iPhone with another person, "For You" will also suggests music which will be influenced by the type of songs that individual plays. If you do not want your songs having an impact on your song recommendations, you can change that by going to Settings, select Music, then disable the "Use Listening History" option.

Update Genre and Artist Inclinations

To update and probably add to your list of genres and artists, Tap for You, tap the contact icon, next, swipe up and select View Account, then tap Choose Artists for You.

Library

The Library tab incorporates any included or downloaded music from Apple Music, music, and music videos synchronized to the iPhone, movies, and other films you included from Apple Music, and iTunes purchases.

Sort your Music

Sorting your music playlist makes it arranged and organized in a fashion that satisfies you. Tap Playlists, Albums, or Songs, then Tap Sort.

Play Music Shared on a Close-by PC

If a PC on your network connection shares music through iTunes Home Sharing, visit Settings, select Music, then tap Sign In under Home Sharing. Come back to the Music application, Tap the Library tab, then tap the Home Sharing option, and choose a shared library.

Expel Apple Music Songs from iPhone

Go to Settings on your iPhone, select Music, and disable iCloud Music Library. The songs are expelled from your iPhone; however, they stay in iCloud. Furthermore, the music you purchased, or those you synchronized also stays intact

Include from Apple Music

To improve your library by adding music to it from Apple Music, do any of these:

-Touch and hold your touch on a song, music collection, playlist, or video, then tap Add to Library.

- When viewing what an album or playlist entails, tap "Add" to include the item or tap the add icon close to each song.

-On the Now Playing screen, tap the add icon.

Add Music to a Playlist

Touch and hold a song collection, playlist, or music video. Tap Add to a Playlist, then select a playlist for the item to be added.

The first time you tap Add to Playlist, you can decide to consequently include songs to your library when you add them to a playlist. If you do this, those songs are accessible in your Library. Go to Settings, select Music, then tap on Add Playlist Songs to enable or disable this setting

Delete Music from Library

Touch and hold the item (which could be a song, an album, playlist, or music video), then tap Delete from Library.

Download music from Apple Music

After adding a song, collection, or playlist, tap the cloud download icon. For this process of downloading to go on with ease, you must enable iCloud Music Library to download music from the Apple Music to your library (go to Settings, select Music, here, enable the iCloud Music Library).

Regulate Music Storage

Perhaps your iPhone is low on storage space, you can evacuate downloaded music that you haven't played in w while. Go to Settings, select tap on Music, and select Optimize Storage.

Delete Music and Videos Stored on your iPhone

To remove a video or music item, touch and hold a song, collection, playlist, music video, TV show, or film. Tap Remove, then tap Remove Downloads. The item is expelled from iPhone, however, not from the iCloud Music Library.

To delete all songs or songs from specific artists from iPhone, go to Settings, select Music, then tap on Downloaded Music this provides you with a rundown of options from which you tap Edit, then tap the remove icon close to All Songs or the artists whose music you intend to delete.

Search for Music

For easy and quick access to a particular item in your library, you can search your library for the item, simply tap the search field, then select "Your Library," then enter an item that you want to search for, select a result from whatever is displayed to you to play that result.

Play Music

Control Playback

To play a song, tap on it, while playing the song, tap on it to display the player. Tapping the leads, you to the Now Playing screen, where you can:

-Tap the play icon to play the song

-Tap the pause icon to stop the playing song.

-Tap the fast forward icon to skip the player to the next song in the sequence.

-Tap the rewind icon to come back to the beginning of the song. Also

double-tapping the rewind icon causes the previous song in a playlist or an album.

Rapidly Navigate to the Album

To swiftly navigate to an album, tap the song, artist, or the album itself in Now Playing.

Conceal Now Playing

To prevent your Now Playing from being displayed, tap the downward directional arrow which is shown at the highest point of the Now Playing screen.

Share Music

Tap the more icon (indicated by three dots), then tap Share Song.

Shuffle

To muddle and mix your playlist so that songs are played at random and not in their sequential order of arrangement, swipe up and tap the shuffle icon, then tap the shuffle icon again to disable shuffling. However, if what you are viewing happens to be a playlist or collection, tap Shuffle All.

Repeat

To rehash the songs in your playlist, tap the Repeat button. Double-tap the button to repeat a just a song. To increase the content in your library by adding songs to it, tap the add icon.

View Lyrics

To view the lyrics of a song as you listen and even while streaming the song, tap the lyrics icon that is displayed at the lower part of the Now Playing screen to view the Lyrics. To return to the Now Playing screen and to conceal the lyrics, tap the lyrics icon. However, not all songs are provided with lyrics.

Access Extra Options

To display additional options in the now playing screen, tap the more icon.

See What's Next in the Queue

To view what's next in line in the Now Playing screen, tap the horizontal bar icon. To view audio controls from the Lock screen or when utilizing another application, bring in the iPhone control center.

Stream Music to a Bluetooth or Airplay-enabled Gadget

In the Now Playing screen, tap emitter icon, then choose a gadget.

▶	Play the current song.
❚❚	Pause playback.
▶▶	Skip to the next song. Touch and hold to fast-forward through the current song.
◀◀	Return to the song's beginning. Tap again to play the previous song in an album or playlist. Touch and hold to rewind through the current song.
—	Hide the Now Playing Screen button.
•••	Tap for more options.

Show time-synced lyrics (lyrics not available for all songs).

 Stream music to Bluetooth or AirPlay-enabled devices.

 See the Playing Next queue.

For You

Here, you get access to playlists compiled by Apple Music experts, collections based on your preferences, and music your companions are listening to.

Mention to Apple Music what you love

Touch and hold your touch on an item in music, then tap to indicate if you Love or Dislike the song. On the Now Playing screen, tap the more icon, then select either Love or Dislike. Mentioning your preferences improves future suggestions.

Creating Frequently Played Collection

Certain albums have a star icon placed close to the most played songs of the moment.

Listening in on your Friends

Provided you're an Apple Music member, you can view the songs that your companions are listening to, however you have to follow them to be able to do this. You can also glance at the playlists they've shared and the music they tune in to regularly. In like manner, your followers can view your common playlists and the music you listen to the most.

Creating a Profile

When you open Music, you're required to set up a profile. Tap Get Started to initiate the process. If you would prefer not to set up a profile at that moment, you can set it up later. Simply tap "For You," tap the contact icon and proceed to tap "Start Sharing with Friends."

Follow your Friends

There are a few different ways to follow individuals:

-Include friends when you set up your profile.

-Swipe to the base of the profile screen, tap Find More Friends, then tap the follow icon close to those you need to follow.

- Tap a profile picture, then tap Follow.

- Tap Search, enter a companion's name, tap it in the outcomes, then tap Follow.

- Tap a suggested companion in For You, then Tap Follow.

A few profiles may show up with a lock on the profile picture, which implies that you have to request and get authorization from that individual to become a follower. When your request has been acknowledged, you see their mutual playlists and the music they're tuning in to.

React to Follow Requests

To respond to requests from people who want to follow you, on the profile screen, tap Follow Requests, then accept or decline the friend request. You get follow requests if you make choices of those who can follow you.

Follow requests may get to you via several ways such as a link in your mail or a text message, to react to do this, tap the link.

Quit Following

Touch and hold the profile image of an individual you follow, then tap Unfollow.

Block Followers

Touch and hold your touch on the profile image of the follower, then tap Block. Individuals you block won't see your music or have the option to find your profile. They can in any case still listen to your mutual playlists If they added them to their library.

Share Music with Followers

Set up a playlist, your followers will be granted access to your playlist in For You on their gadgets except you have disabled "Show on My Profile." If you make alterations to the songs you share, those alterations are effected on your followers' devices.

Change your Mutual Playlists

On the profile screen, tap Edit, then enable or disable the playlist, then drag the horizontal bars to reorder the songs on your playlist.

Monitoring your Follower's Music Interest

To view what others are listening to, tap For You, then tap an individual's profile picture to view shared playlists and songs often listened to. Furthermore, you can also view their followers and the individuals they follow.

Share your Profile

On the profile screen, tap the More option, then select Share Profile, then select a sharing option. You can also share the profile of anybody you follow, or who follows you.

See Who You're Following

On the profile screen, swipe up to view the individuals you're following and the individuals who are following you.

Report an Issue

If you have a worry about a follower, touch and hold their profile image, then tap Report a Concern.

Playlists

Create Playlists to Arrange your Music

This enables you to organize the songs in your library into different sections. Tap Library, then tap Playlists and select a new playlist. Input a title and depiction, tap Add Music to select the songs to be added to the playlist.

You can tap the More icon in a list of songs or on the Now Playing screen, followed by tapping Add to a Playlist, then tap New Playlist.

Customize your Playlist's Artwork

Tap Edit, then tap the camera icon, to complete this change, snap a picture or select an image from your photo library.

Share Playlist with Non-Followers

Touch and hold a playlist, a lot of options will be displayed, tap Share Playlist

Set up a Public Playlist

Select a playlist you made, tap Edit, then enable Public Playlist.

Rename Playlist

Select the playlist, tap Edit, and input the name, these allow you to include more songs, delete a delete, alter song order. Recent and changed playlists are added to iCloud Music Library and show up on all your gadgets if you're registered as an Apple Music member. In case you're not a member, they're duplicated to your music library whenever you synchronize the iPhone with your computer.

Remove Playlist

To get rid of a playlist from your library, touch and hold the playlist, then tap "Delete from Library."

Explore Recently Played Songs

Browse the content of the music app to obtain recommendations for good music, playlist, and more, just to ensure that you derive utility. Tap the Browse tab, and Tap "New Music."

Browse Playlists Compiled by Experts

In the Music app, tap Playlists, then pick a playlist, action, genre, etc.

Watch select TV Shows and Films

Tap "TV and Movies," then select a movie and tap on it to play it. However, TV shows and movies pictures aren't accessible in all locations.

View What's Trending

Tap Top Charts, the top songs of the moment will be displayed to you, then choose a song, album, music video, or artist.

Browse Preferred Genres

Tap Genres, choose from the results, then tap a song, album, or any featured item to enjoy songs that were carefully selected by music experts.

Radio

The most important component here is Beats 1, which features international-level radio shows, the most recent music, and exclusive discussions. You can also tune in to embedded stations that have been created by music specialists. Also, you can make consuetude stations from songs or artists you pick.

Tune in to Live Radio

Tap the presently playing program on Beats 1. However, since Beats 1 is live radio, you can't interfere with song playbacks such as pausing, skipping, or rewinding songs.

Tune in to past shows and discover when your preferred shows are on. Tap Beats 1, then tap a show or DJ.

Setup a Station

Touch and hold an artist or song, then tap Create Station.

Fine-tune Your Stations

While playing a station you made, tap the Player to show the Now Playing screen, tap the star icon, then select Play More Like This or Play Less Like This.

Siri and Voice Control

You can utilize Siri or Voice Control to direct music playback. Also, Siri can assist you with discovering music in the iTunes Store.

Use Siri

To bring in Siri, Tap and hold the home button on your iPhone. Siri is compatible with several commands, which you can put into use the following ways:

Play a Song, Video, and Other Items: Say "play," then you pronounce the name of the song, collection, artist, or station that you intend to play. Perhaps Siri doesn't find what you requested, be more explicit. For instance, "play the radio station 'High Vibes" as opposed to stating "play 'High Vibes.'"

Play Similar Music: While music is playing and you want to hear more songs with a similar genre, simply say "play more tunes this way one" or "create a radio broadcast dependent on this song "

Pick music depending on your mood: Say something like "play something cheerful" or "play some perky music."

Let Siri be your DJ: Say something like "play something I like," "play suggested music," "play an album I like"

Request more details: You can ask Siri for details about a song or album, details such as the year the song was released, its position on the billboard charts, and so on.

Add music from Apple Music to your collection: To include songs these songs, simply say "add, then you say the title of the song and any other information about the song that makes it easy to locate' to my Library."

Add a song or collection to a playlist: To include a song to a playlist While listening to the song, say something like "add this song to my reading playlist."

Correct Siri: If Siri doesn't play what you hope to hear, say something like "No, the track by Drake " or "No, the cover by Jimmy."

More Advanced Sound Settings

Check, Equalization

Select an equalization (EQ) setting

Go to Settings, tap Music, then select EQ. Equalization settings apply just to music played from the Music application, yet they influence all sound output.

Set a Volume Limit

Go to Settings, tap Music, select Volume Limit. To prevent further manipulation to the volume limit, go to Settings, select General, then tap Restrictions. Choose Volume Limit, then tap Don't Allow Changes.

Normalize the Volume Level of your Sound

Go to Settings, select Music, then enable Sound Check

Chapter Twenty-One

Managing your Mails with your iPhone

Compose a message

Tap the compose icon, the text box comes up, then enter your message. To view draft messages touch and hold the compose icon. Siri can also be useful when it comes to composing messages on mail, you can summon Siri and say words like "Email John and say I received the order, thank you."

Include drawings to your Message

To include drawings or sketches into your message, double-tap the message box, tap Insert Drawing, then utilize the drawing and annotation tools. Tap Done to embed the drawing into your message.

Add Attachments to Messages

To include attachments such as links, documents, or files, double-tap in the message body, then tap Add Attachment. Here, select a document or whatever it is that you want to attach.

Insert a Picture or Video

Double-tap the message box, and tap Insert Photo or Video.

Quote some Content when you Reply

To quote a text or a portion of the text, touch and hold on the message body, then select the content you intend to quote. Tap the reply icon, then tap Reply and that does it. To disable indentation of the cited content, go to Settings, tap on Mail, then select Increase Quote Level.

Send a Message from an Alternate Account

Tap the "From" field to pick an account, then enter the message and send it.

Change a Receiver from Carbon copy (Cc) to Blind Carbon copy (Bcc)

After you enter recipients of the message, you can drag them, starting with one field, then onto the next, or change their sequence.

Mark Addresses Outside Specific Spaces

When you're tending to a message from a receiver who's not in your domain, you can have the receiver's name hued in red to prompt you. Go to Settings, tap Mail, select Mark Addresses, and state the domains that you intend not to be marked. You can input numerous domains segregated by commas. for example, "common.org, apple.com, book.org."

Include Extra Mail Accounts

Go to Settings, tap Accounts and Passwords, then tap Include Account. Select Other, then choose Add Mail Account.

Change your Mail Signature

Go to Settings > Mail > Signature. Perhaps you have more than one mail account, tap "Per Account" to set an alternate signature for every one of them.

Automatically Send Yourself a Duplicate

Enable Settings, then go to Mail and tap on "Always Bcc Myself."

Preview your Mail Messages

To view a better preview of your messages, go to Settings, tap Mail, select Preview. With this mode of preview, you can view about five lines.

Determine Messages Met for You

Go to Settings, tap Mail, then enable "Show To/Cc Labels. In the mail message list, a tag close to your name defines how it was addressed to you. You can also utilize the To/Cc mailbox, which accumulates all mail meant for you. To view or conceal it, tap Mailboxes, then tap Edit.

View Other Messages While Composing a Mail

Swipe down on the title bar of a message you're composing. When you intend to come back to your message, tap its title at the base of the screen. Perhaps you have multiple messages yet to be completed, tap the base of the screen to view them all.

Save Draft for Future Use

In case you're composing a message and you decide to complete it later, tap Cancel, then tap Save Draft. To retrieve the message, touch, and hold the compose icon.

Receive Notifications from Message Responses

While reading a message, tap the flag icon, then tap "Notify Me." While you're composing a message, tap the notification icon in the Subject field. To change how notifications, show up, go to Settings, tap Notifications, select Mail, then tap "Thread Notifications."

Gather Significant Messages

Add notable individuals to your VIP list so that all their messages show up in the VIP mailbox. When viewing a message, tap Details, tap the sender's name to display their contact information, then Tap "Add to VIP." To alter how notifications are displayed, go to Settings, select Notifications, tap Mail, then tap VIP.

Furthermore, Siri can assist you with mails, make a statement like: "Any recent mail from John today?"

Flag Messages for Easy Future Reference

Tap the flag icon while perusing the message. To change the display of the flagged message, go to Settings > Mail > Flag Style. To view the Flagged letterbox, tap Edit while going through the mailboxes list, then tap Flagged.

Search for a Message

Scroll to the top of the message rundown to uncover the search field, then input the content you're searching for. Select between searching the entire mailboxes or the present mailbox at the top of the results list. Tap a message in the result rundown to view it, then tap directional arrows to go through the different messages. The searching process puts into consideration the address fields, the subject, and the content of the message.

Search by Time Allotment

Scroll the page to the top of the messages rundown to uncover the search field, and input something like "April meeting" to bring out all messages from April with "meeting."

Search by Message Type

To locate all flagged, unread messages from individuals in your VIP list, input "Flag unread VIP." You can also locate other message properties, for example, "attachments."

Get Rid of Junks in Mail

Tap the flag icon while you're perusing a message, then tap "Move to Junk" to place it in the Junk folder. If you coincidentally move a message, shake the iPhone quickly to undo.

Display All your Draft Messages

While checking the mailbox list, tap Edit, then tap Add Mailbox, then Enable "All Draft" in the mailbox.

View a Message

Tap a message to view it. To delete it, tap the trash icon. To enable or disable the affirmation that the item has been deleted, go to Settings, tap Mail, select Ask Before Deleting.

Remove a Message with a Swipe

While checking through a list of messages, swipe a message slightly to the left side of the screen to display a list of actions, then tap Delete. Alternatively, to delete a message just with single gesture control, swipe the message totally to the left side of the screen.

Retrieve a Deleted Message

To restore mail messages that have been deleted, go to the account's Trash mailbox, open the message, then tap the folder icon and move the message. To view deleted messages on all your accounts, including the "All Trash mailbox." To include it, tap Edit in the letterboxes list, then select it in the list.

Archive Rather than Delete

Rather than erasing messages, you can archive them so they're still accessible in the Archive mailbox, supposing you need them. The method of enabling this feature depends on the type of mail account you have set up. Go to Settings, tap Mail, select Accounts, choose [account name]. When it comes to advanced settings, change the destination mailbox for the junked messages to "Archive".

After you have enabled this option, to delete a message as opposed to archiving it, touch and hold the archive icon, then tap Trash Message.

Stash your trash messages

You can set the extent to which deleted messages remain in the Trash mailbox. Go to Settings, tap Mail, select Accounts, select [account name], tap Advanced, then choose "Remove." Some email services may supersede your selections; for instance, iCloud doesn't store deleted messages for more than 30 days, regardless of whether you selected the "Never" option.

Handling Attachments

View an Attachment

Touch and hold the attachments, then Tap Quick Look.

Save a Picture or Video to Photos

If a received message includes pictures or videos, touch and holds the item, then tap Quick Look. Tap the Share icon, then choose Save Image.

Mark-up an Attachment

Use Mark-up to comment on a picture or a PDF attachment. To do this, touch and hold the item, then tap Mark-up (if it's an attachment that you intend to send), or "Mark-up and Reply" then utilize the drawing and annotation tool.

View an Attachment with a Different Application

Several applications on the iPhone can be used to view an attachment sent as a mail message. Touch and hold the attachment until a menu is displayed, then tap the application you intend to use to open the attachment. A few attachments consequently display an option you can use to open other applications.

View Messages with Attachments

Tap the filtering icon to enable filtering, proceed by tapping on "Filtered by" and enable "Only Mail with Attachments." You can as well utilize the Attachments mailbox, which displays messages with attachments from all accounts. To include it, tap Edit while checking through the Mailboxes list.

Send Enormous Attachments

Mail Drop allows you to send documents that surpass the maximum size permitted by your email account. Tap Send whenever you intend to send a message with huge attachments, then adhere to the on-screen guidelines to use Mail Drop.

Manage Message with a Swipe

While checking through a rundown of messages, slightly swipe a message to the left side to uncover several actions. You can as well swipe a message to the right side to uncover another action. Select the options you want to show up in the menus in Settings > Mail > Swipe Options.

Organize your Mail with Letter Drops

Tap Edit in the letterboxes list to make another one, or rename, or delete one. Some implicit letterboxes can't be changed. There are certain smart mailboxes, for example, Unread, that display messages from all your accounts. Tap the ones you need to utilize.

See the Entire Discussion

Go to Settings > Mail, then enable Organize by Thread. Swipe a message in a thread right or left to display several options. To alter the way threads are displayed, go to Settings > Mail. To manipulate the swipe settings, go to Settings > Mail > Swipe Options.

Filter Messages

Tap the filter icon to conceal messages that don't fit into the present filter. Tap the filter icon again to disable the filter option. You can filter through certain requirements such as by reading or flagged status, by messages directed to you, messages from VIPs, and so on.

View and Save Addresses

While perusing the message, tap Details at the top of the message.

Add somebody to Contacts or make them a VIP

Tap the individual's name or email address, then select "Add to VIP." You can also add the location to a recent or existing contact.

Print Messages

Tap the reply icon, then tap "Print" in the list of options.

-Print an attachment or picture. Tap the to view it, then tap the reply icon and select "Print."

Block Senders

In case you block contact with an email, it will consequently block messages from them too.

You can also do this from the Mail application. Go to the mall app and tap on the profile icon of the sender. Select the email address or name of the sender, this will display the sender's title card. From here, choose "Block this contact." On the preceding screen, affirm this step.

Chapter Twenty-Two

Managing your Calendar

Include an Event

In day view in the calendar app, touch and hold time until a new event shows up, then fill in the event subtleties. If you include the location of the event, you will be reminded to embark early for your journey based on your present location, given the traffic conditions.

Search for Events

To inquire about events, tap the search icon, then input the search text in the search field provided. The titles, invitees, areas, and notes for the schedules that are being displayed are searched.

Ask Siri

To bring in Siri's assistance in the calendar app, summon Siri and make a statement like: "Where is my 4 pm meeting?" "Set up a meeting with Tracy by 9 am," "When is my next meeting."

To access the display of your weekly schedule in the calendar, turn the iPhone sideways.

To alter your view in calendar, tap a year, month, or day option to enable you to zoom in the app or zoom it out. When fixed in the week or day view, pinch the screen to zoom it in or out.

To access a rundown of occasions in the calendar, in the month view, tap the events icon to display a day's event.

Adjust an Event

Adjusting your events could mean rescheduling, touch and hold the event, then drag it to another time, or alter the grab points. Also, you can make use of Siri here by making statements like "Reschedule my appointment with Joyce to next Friday at 3 pm."

Set a Default Schedule

Go to Settings, tap Calendar, go further to select Default Calendar. When you include an event utilizing Siri or utilizing different applications, it's included in your default Calendar.

Tweak Calendar

Go to Settings, tap Calendar to set which day of the week schedule begins with, show week numbers, make choices of an alternate calendar, abrogate the programmed time zone, and lots more.

Invite Others to an Event

You can choose to include more individuals to an occasion, regardless of whether you're the person who planned it or not, with Exchange and a few other servers. Select an event, tap Edit, then tap Invitees. Input names or tap to select individuals from Contacts. If you prefer not to be notified when somebody rejects a meeting, go to Settings, tap Calendar, then disable "Show Invitee Declines."

Rapidly Send an Email to Event Participants

Tap the event, Tap Invitees, then tap the message icon.

Propose a Different Meeting Time

You can propose another time for a meeting invitation you've gotten. Select the meeting, then Tap Propose New Time. Contingent upon the capacities of your calendar server, the coordinator will get either a contrasting proposal or an email of your proposition.

Display Several Calendars Simultaneously

To view multiple calendars at the same time, tap Calendars, then pick the calendars you intend to see.

Enable iCloud, Google, Exchange, or Yahoo! Calendars

Enabling the calendars of these servers permits you to carry out more activities with the calendar. Go to Settings, tap Accounts and Passwords, select Add Account, then choose Other, tap "Add CalDAV Account or Add subscribed Calendar," then enter a server address.

Subscribing to a Calendar

Subscribing provides you with up to date information and notifies you about the calendar. Go to Settings > Accounts and

Passwords > Add Accounts > Other, then tap Add Subscribed Calendar. Input the URL of the .ics of the item you intend to subscribe to. Furthermore, you can as well subscribe to an iCalendar (.ics) schedule by tapping a link that leads you to the calendar.

To merge a CalDAV account with your calendar, go to Settings, tap Accounts and Passwords, then select "Add Record," go further to tap "Other," then select Add CalDAV account. If the account you want to use happens to be a macOS Server account, select "Add macOS Server Account."

Chapter Twenty-Three

Overview of the Photos App

The photos application provides you with an avenue to see, sort out, share, and edit your media items.

There are numerous approaches to get pictures and videos on iPhone, you can: take them with your iPhone's Camera, enable iCloud pictures Library to match up all your media items on all your iOS devices, synchronize them with iTunes from your PC, bring the items in from a camera, save the items from an email or a site page, and many other ways. Furthermore, you can as well view animated GIFs on the photos app.

Display and work with your pictures in the Photos, For You, Album and Search tabs at the base of the screen.

-The Photos tab contains all your still pictures, Live pictures, and videos, sorted into four subsections which are: Years, Months, Days, and All Photos. These are time-based subsections that contain pictures that were taken or videos that were made in a particular year, month, or day put into the same groups. To rapidly go through pictures in any of these categories, Tap and hold a thumbnail, then drag it, if you come across a picture that you want to view, tap the thumbnail to view it.

-For You tab keeps records of events of a particular day, for instance, if individuals with birthday details in your contacts have pictures in your gallery, a special birthday gallery will be displayed on their birthday in "For You". Also, the For You tab displays your best memories and happy moments based on events that occurred or the places you visited.

-The album tab enables you to set up your albums and view them.

-The Search tab provides you with quick access to an item. You can search for items by using time-based references e.g. April 2017, or location-based references such as Amusement park, stadium, etc.

Browse your Gallery

Select a category in the Photos app, then tap on a picture or video. While glancing at a picture, swipe the thumbnail to go through items in that category, while checking through, if you come across an item you want to view, tap the thumbnail. Drag down the item to keep perusing the photo's category.

Zoom in or Out

Tap twice on an item or pinch the item in or out, drag the zoomed item to view its different parts.

Play a Slideshow

While glancing at photograph or video, tap the Share icon, then tap Slideshow. To halt the slideshow, touch the screen, then tap the pause icon shown on the screen. Tap Options to pick a slideshow background display, music, and more. Moreover, with Airplay Mirroring, you can stream a slideshow or video on your iPhone SE2 to a television.

Play a Live Photo

A Live Photo is a feature on the iPhone that captures the moments just before and after the image is captured. In full screen in the Photos app, Tap and hold the Live Photo option to view its movement. To edit a live video, open the live video, and tap "Edit," this provides you with the options of setting a key photo, setting up a still picture, cropping a live video, and muting a live video.

Add Effects to a Live Picture

You can swipe up on the picture to include Live Photo effects which are:

-Loop: reiterates the action in a steady looping video.

-Bounce: retracts the action backward and forward.

-Long Exposure: imitates an exposure like DSLR by blurring motion.

View Photo and Video Subtleties

Touch the item, and swipe up to see:

- Related recollections
- Individuals distinguished by Photos
- Place or Location where the photo or video was taken.

Organize Photos and Videos

The Albums tab incorporates albums you create yourself and those that Photos make for you, depending on the type of pictures or videos. For instance, pictures you take with the forward-facing FaceTime camera are consequently added to the Selfies album. Several albums that Photos creates incorporate Favorites, Peoples, Spots, Live Photographs, Recordings, Scenes, Slo-mo, Screen captures, and more.

If the iCloud Photo Library is what you use, all your pictures are displayed in the All Photos album, also in the Photos Tab. Else, you see the Camera which entails the pictures and videos you took with your iPhone and from different sources. Using the iCloud Photo Library stores your album in iCloud. They're updated and accessible on devices where the same Apple ID is used to log in to iCloud.

Create an Album

Tap the album tab, then tap the add icon.

Select either to set up a New Album or a New Shared Album.

Input the name of the album, then Tap Save.

Select the pictures and videos you want to include in the album, then tap Done.

Add Items to Current Album

To include pictures and videos to an album, Tap the Photos tab at the base of the Photos app screen, then tap Select. Tap the thumbnails of the items you intend to add to the album and Tap the share icon. Swipe up and Tap "Add to Album" in the list of options, then select the album you intend to add it to.

-Delete an Album: tap the remove icon on an album. However, you can't delete albums that Photos itself makes for you, for example, Peoples, Places, and Selfies. After making any alterations in the album tab, tap Done to effect the changes.

Hide Pictures or Videos

While going through the thumbnails, tap Select to choose the items you intend to hide, tap the Share icon, then tap Hide. The items are transferred to the hidden album. Pictures and videos selected to be hidden are hidden from other categories, but visible in the Album tab.

Deleting from Photos

Tap a tab in photos to display pictures and videos it contains, tap picture or video, tap the trash icon, then Tap Delete Photo or Delete Video. Deleted items are kept in the "Recently Deleted" album for a period of 30 days before they're permanently expelled from the iPhone. However, you can check the number of days remaining for the item to be permanently deleted from the iPhone.

To delete a picture or video permanently from the Recently Deleted album before the 30-day validity period is reached, tap the item in the album, then tap Delete. If you use iCloud Photograph Library, deleted items are permanently expelled from every one of your gadgets that use iCloud Photo Library with the same Apple ID.

Restore a Deleted Picture or Video

In the "Recently Deleted" album, tap the picture or video, tap Recover. Then select Recover Picture or Recover Video to transfer the item to the Camera Roll or, in case you use iCloud Photo Library, they are transferred to the All Photos album. To recoup various photos and videos, tap the "Recently Deleted" album, tap "Select", pick the items you intend to recoup, then tap Recover.

Remove a Picture or Video from an Album

Tap the item, tap the trash icon. You can decide to expel it from the album or delete it from your iCloud Photo Library on the entirety of your devices

Memories

Photos check your library to consequently set up collections of pictures and videos called Memories. Memories can incorporate Memory movies, which are consequently edited for you and set up with a soundtrack. You can alter their features and share them with others. However, Memories made from collections that do not contain enough pictures and videos won't produce a Memory film. You can also make a Memory film from the collections you make.

Memories can be based on:

- Locations, for example, a preferred vacation spot or your neighborhood.
- Extraordinary events, for example, birthday events, occasions, weddings, exhibitions.
- Activities, for example, climbing, skiing, and plunging.
- Pictures of family, companions, small children, and pets

Play a Memory film

Tap the "For You" tab, then select Memory, tap a memory film to play it. To interrupt the movie, tap the film, then tap the pause icon. To flip between the portrait and landscape mode while viewing the film, rotate your iPhone.

View a Collection's Memory

Tap an album you set up, then tap the side direction arrow icon. To include it in Memories, swipe up on the album, then Tap "Add to Memories."

To include a memory to the Favorite Memories collection, Tap and hold a memory, then tap Add to Favorite Memories.

To create Memories based on events from holiday, go to Settings, tap Photos, then enable "Show Holiday Events."

Change the Mood of a Movie

The customization settings allow you to change the mood of the movie, to do this, tap a Memory film while it's playing, and select a mood. Or then again, swipe the moods left or right to pick another one. Each mood incorporates a title, music, and editing style.

Alter the Duration

Tap a Memory film while it's playing, and select a duration or swipe to pick short, medium, or long. All durations may not be accessible for every film.

Customize a Memory film

Tap a Memory film while it's playing, and select tap Edit to carry out the following:

Change the Title

Tap Title, tap the title and caption to alter them, then select a title format.

Select a Title Picture

Tap Title Image, go further to select a picture or video you want to use.

Select Another Music

Tap Music, then select music from a soundtrack or your music library, only the music that is saved on your iPhone is available for use here.

-To select a custom duration, select Duration from the options.

Select Pictures and Videos

Tap Photos and Videos in the list of options, tap the add icon, then tap the photos and recordings you need in the film. Deselect items you have in the Memory film to expel them.

Delete an Item from the Memory Film

Tap the Photos and Videos option, then select an item, and tap the trash icon to expel it from the movie.

Trim a video in the Memory film

Tap the Photos and Videos option, select a video in the timeline, then trim the video.

Managing Individuals

Photos check your picture library for individuals' faces and add the usually found faces to the Peoples collection. You can tag names to the people Photos finds, include individuals who show up less often, select individuals as Favorites, and display memories that contain certain individuals. The more items you have, the longer the time a first search requires.

Name an Individual

Select the album, then tap people, and choose a person. Tap the name box at the crest of the screen, then input a name, or select the name in the list, if it shows up. Tap Next, then tap Done.

Mark Individuals as Favorites

In the album, on an individual's key image, tap the heart icon, this includes the individual into your list of favorites. You can as well drag an individual to the Favorites area.

To remove several favorites simultaneously, tap Select, select the people you need to expel, then tap Unfavorite.

Merge Individuals

In case a person in the People album is recognized as two or more people, tap Select, select each instance of the individual, then tap Merge.

Set an Individual's Key Picture

Tap the individual's collection, Tap Select, then pick the picture you intend to use as the key photo. Tap the Share icon, then tap "Make Key Photo."

View Photographs that Contain an Individual.

Open the album, tap People, then select the individual.

Places

The Places album sets up collections of your pictures and videos dependent on where they were taken. Collections are shown on a map inside the album. Only pictures and videos that are provided with location details (GPS information) are incorporated.

View Items by Location

Open Albums, Tap Places, then choose a collection. Zoom in on the map provided in the album to view more precise locations.

See a Rundown of Locations

While looking at the map, tap Grid.

View an area in the Maps application

When a picture or video that entails location details is displayed, swipe up to view places, then select the location's name or address.

View a Location-based Memory film

Open Albums, select Places, pick a location that has several pictures it entails, proceed, then tap the play icon.

iCloud Photograph Library

iCloud Photo Library exigently uploads the pictures and videos you take and saves them in their original configuration at full resolution in iCloud. You can access your items in the iCloud Photo Library from any gadget where you've signed in with the same Apple ID. Also, if you use the Photos app to open and edit your pictures and videos, the changes are made on all your gadgets.

However, it is important to know that if you enable iCloud Photo Library, your ability to use iTunes to synchronize photos and videos to iPhone will become restricted.

-**Enable iCloud Photo Library:** Go to Settings> [your name] > iCloud > Photos, alternatively, you can enable it in the Photos section in Settings.

Improve Storage or Pictures and Videos in Full Resolution

By default, the "Optimize iPhone Storage" option has been enabled. It manages space on iPhone by consequently storing your full-resolution photos and videos in iCloud and smaller renditions optimized for iPhone. To retain the full-resolution originals on your iPhone, go to Settings > [your name] > iCloud > Photos, then select Download and Keep Originals.

Download a Full Resolution Item

In case you're not saving full-resolution forms on your iPhone, pinch the screen to zoom in to 100%, or tap Edit. The full-resolution picture or video then starts to download by itself. To use your cellular data to upload and download from iCloud Photo Library all the time, go to Settings > Photographs > Cellular Data, then enable Unlimited Updates. In an instance whereby you exceed your storage plan, you can increase your iCloud storage. Go to Settings > [your name] > iCloud. Tap Manage Storage, then tap Upgrade.

My Photo Stream

My Photo Stream consequently uploads your latest pictures to iCloud, so you can access them on devices that aren't operating on the iCloud Photo Library. However, it doesn't transmit Live Pictures or videos. Items in My Photo Stream do not place any restriction on iCloud storage, and they're temporarily saved for 30 days in iCloud. Download the items to your device if you intend to save them permanently.

Enable or Disable My Photo Stream

Go to Settings, tap [your name], select iCloud, tap Photos, then enable or disable "Upload to My Photo Stream."

Use My Photo Stream without iCloud Photo Library

Pictures taken with your iPhone are included in the My Photo Stream collection when you leave the Camera application and your iPhone has an active Wi-Fi connection. Any pictures you include additionally show up in your My Photo Stream album. Furthermore, items included in My Photo Stream on your other gadgets automatically show up in your My Photo Stream collection on iPhone.

Save Photos from My Photo Stream to your iPhone

Pictures in My Photo Stream are retained in iCloud for 30 days after which they are removed. To retain these pictures, you have to save them from My Photo Stream to your iPhone.

-Tap the album tab and tap My Photo Stream.

-Tap Select, then choose the pictures you intend to save.

-Tap the share icon, then tap Save Image.

Delete pictures: Select the pictures, then tap the trash icon.

Even though deleted pictures are removed from My Photo Stream on all your gadgets, the original pictures are retained in the Photos app on the device on which they were taken. Also, pictures that have been saved to another album on a device or computer aren't deleted.

iCloud Photograph Sharing

With iCloud Photo Sharing, you can entreat other people who are also using iCloud Photo Sharing to see your pictures and videos. You can also exhibit your collections on a website for anybody to see. iCloud Photo Sharing performs its duty with or without iCloud Photo Library and My Photo Stream.

To put iCloud Photo Sharing to use, your iPhone must have an Internet connection, cellular data charges may apply.

Enable iCloud Photo Sharing

Go to Settings > [your name] >iCloud >Photos, then enable iCloud Photos.

Share Pictures and Videos

While glancing at a picture or video, or after choosing different pictures or videos, Tap the share icon, select iCloud Photo Sharing, include comments, then share to an existing shared album or set up another one. You can entreat individuals to check your shared album using the email address or the mobile telephone number they use to get text messages.

Enable a Public Website

Tap Shared, select an album, tap People, then enable Public website. Tap the "Share link" option if you want to make the site known to others.

Enable Shared Albums

Go to Settings > [your name] >iCloud >Photos, then enable shared album.

Create New Shared Album

Open the albums tab and tap the ads icon. Select "New Shared Album" and input a name for it. Choose the people to invite from your contacts, or type in an email address or iMessage phone number, then tap Create.

Include Items to Shared Album

Tap Shared, select the album, tap the add icon, then choose the items, and tap Done. You can include a remark, then tap Post.

Remove Pictures from a Shared Album

Tap Shared, select an album, tap Select, choose the pictures that you intend to delete, then tap the trash icon. The shares album or pictures must be owned by you.

Delete Remarks from a Shared Album

Tap the photograph or video that bears the remark. Tap the comment area at the base of the screen, touch and hold the remark, then tap Delete. The shared album must be yours or comments should be made by you.

Rename a Shared Album.

Tap Shared, tap edit, then tap the name and input another one.

To add or remove subscribers, as well as enable or disable notifications, select the shared album, then Tap People.

Subscribe to a Shared Album

When you obtain an invitation, tap the shared tab, then acknowledge the invitation by tapping "Accept." You can as well accept an invitation in an email.

Expel a Subscriber

Tap the shared album, then go to the Peoples tab. Select a subscriber that you intend to remove and tap "Remove Subscriber."

Add Items to a Subscribed Shared Album

Tap Shared, select an album, then tap the add icon. Choose the items you want to add, then tap done. You can include a comment, the post it. Subscribers of an album can only delete items added by then or comments made by them.

View your Family Album

When Family Sharing is set up, a shared album called Family is created in Photos on all the members' gadgets. Everybody in the family can add pictures, videos, and comments to the album, and be prompted at whatever point something new is included.

How to Delete a Shared Album

Select the shared album, tap on the People tab, then select "Delete Shared Album."

Different Approaches to Share Pictures and Videos

You can share items in Mail or Messages or employing other applications you installed.

-**Share a single picture or video:** Open the picture or video, tap the share icon, then select how you intend to share it.

-Share multiple pictures or videos in All Photos or Days: While looking at the pictures in the All Photos or Days tab, tap Select, then choose the pictures you intend to share. Tap the Share icon, then pick a share option. These pictures can be shared via an iCloud link. The iCloud link remains valid for 30 days and can be shared using any application.

-Share several pictures or videos in Months: While going through the events in the Months, tap the More icon, then tap Share Photos to send all the pictures from that event.

Save or Share an Item you Receive

-From email: tap the item to download it if need be, then tap the Share icon. Alternatively, you can just touch and hold the item, then select a sharing or saving option.

-From a text message: Tap the icon in the discussion, tap the share icon, then select a saving or sharing option.

--Edit and adjust pictures and videos.

Modify Light and Color

In the Photo app, tap a picture or video thumbnail to display it in full screen. Tap Edit, then swipe left under the picture to display the editing buttons for each feature, for example, Exposure, Brilliance, and Highlights. When you tap the Enhance button, it automatically adds effects pictures and videos.

Tap a button, then move the slider to adjust the impact of the feature. The extent of alterations you make for each impact is shown by the outline around the button, so you can immediately see which effects have been increased or diminished. To review the impact, tap the effect button to view the picture before and after the effect was added (or tap the picture to flip between the edited rendition and the original).

Tap Done to save to your changes, or if you are not pleased with the changes, tap Cancel, then Tap Discard Changes.

Crop, Rotate or Flip a Picture

Display the picture in full screen by tapping on its thumbnail. Tap Edit, tap the crop button, this allows you to:

-Crop the image yourself by dragging the edges to encase the areas you intend to retain in the picture, or you can pinch the picture open or closed.

-**Crop to a standard pre-set proportion:** Tap the Standard Crop button, then select a proportion like Square, 2:3, 8:10, and so on.

-**Rotate:** Tap the Rotate button to turn the picture 90 degrees.

-**Flip**: Tap the Flip button to flip the picture on a level plane.

Tap Done to save your alterations, or if you are not satisfied with the changes, tap Cancel, then Tap Discard Changes.

Apply Filter Effects

With the picture displayed in full screen, tap Edit, then tap the Filter button to employ filters effect, for example, Vivid, Dramatic. Select a filter, then move the slider to modify the effect. To compare the edited form of the picture to the original, tap the picture. Tap Done to save your changes or tap Cancel to waive the changes.

Revert an Edited Picture

After editing a picture and saving the changes, you can still change it to the original picture. Open the edited picture, tap Edit, then tap Revert.

Trim a Video

In the Photos app, open the video, then Tap Edit. Move either end of the frame view, then tap Done. Saving a trimmed video provides you with two options, you either:

-Tap Save Video so that only the trimmed video will be saved, or

-Tap Save Video as New Clip so that the two renditions of the video are saved.

To nullify the trim after saving, open the video, tap Edit, then tap Revert. However, a video saved as a new clip can't be transposed to the original.

Mark up a Picture

Select a picture to display it in full screen. Tap Edit, then Tap the More information button. Tap mark up and illustrate the picture using several drawing tools, tap the add icon to include shapes, texts, or even your signature.

Set the Slow-motion Segment of a Video Shot in Slo-mo

In the Slo-mo section, select a video, then tap Edit. Adjust the position of the white vertical bars underneath frame viewer to set where the video is played in slow motion.

Print pictures on iPhone to an AirPrint-enabled printer

-Print a single picture: While displaying a picture in the Photos app, tap the Share button, then tap Print.

-**Print multiple pictures:** While displaying pictures in the Photos app, tap Select, select every picture you intend to print, tap the Share button, then tap Print.

Import Photographs and Recordings on iPhone

You can bring in pictures and videos to the Photos application on your iPhone SE2 from a digital camera, an SD memory card, or another iPhone, or any other device via the Lightning to USB Camera Adapter or the Lightning to SD Card Camera Reader.

Put the camera connector or card reader into the Lightning connector on your iPhone SE2. Then, carry out any of the following:

-Connect a camera: Utilize the USB cable that came with the camera to connect it to the camera connector. Turn on the camera, ensure it has been set to transfer mode. For more details, check the manual that came with the camera.

-Put an SD memory card into the card reader.

-Connect an iPhone, iPad, or iPod touch: Use the USB cable that accompanied the phone to connect it to the camera connector. Turn on and unlock the device.

Having done that, open Photos app on your iPhone, then tap Import.

Select the pictures and videos you intend to import, then select where you want them to be imported to on your iPhone. You can:

-Import all items: Tap Import All.

-Import only a few items: Select the things you intend to import, then tap "Import Selected."

After the items have been imported, you can either retain or delete them on the devices you imported them from (camera, card, iPhone, iPad, or iPod contact). Detach the camera connector or card reader.

Chapter Twenty-Four

Camera App for Snapping a Picture

Photo is the default mode that is displayed when you open the Camera. Swipe left or right to pick an alternate mode, for example, Video, Pano, Time-pass, Slo-mo, and Portrait.

Tap the camera app on the Home screen or swipe left from the Lock screen to open Camera in Photo mode. Tap the Shutter button or Tap either of the volume buttons to snap the picture.

Enable or Disable Flash

Tap the Flash button on the screen, then select your preferred option.

Set a Timer

Fix your shot and balance your iPhone, then tap the Timer button at the top of the screen.

Adjust the Camera's Focus and Exposure

Before you snap a picture, the iPhone camera, by itself, sets the focus, balance, exposure, and adjusts certain effects cross numerous faces. If you need to physically modify these effects, tap the screen to display focus area and exposure settings. Select where you intend to move the focus area, then drag the adjust exposure button to alter the exposure.

Take Low-light Photographs with Night mode

Use Night mode to catch more detail and light up your shots in low-light circumstances. The extent of the exposure in Night mode is resolved consequently, yet you can explore with manual controls. Night mode is activated automatically in low-light situations.

The yellow color displayed by the night mode button at the top of the screen, it indicates that the night mode is on. Furthermore, a number is displayed close to the Night mode button, this indicates how long the camera will take to shoot, tap the Shutter button, and keep the camera still to snap the picture.

To explore with Night mode, tap the Night mode button, then use the slider underneath the frame to pick between the Auto and Max clocks. With Auto, the exposure time is resolved automatically; Max utilizes the longest exposure time.

Take a Live Photo

A Live Photo captures what happens not long before you snap your picture, including the sound. Tap the Live Photo button to activate Live Photos. Then, Tap the Shutter button to take the shot. You can edit Live pictures in Photos. In your collections, Live Photos are indicated with "Live" in the corner.

Take Burst shots

Burst mode takes numerous rapid pictures so you have a scope of pictures to select from. You can take Burst pictures with the back and front cameras. Swipe the shutter button to the left to take rapid shots.

Record a Video

Pick Video mode

Tap the Record button or Tap either of the volume buttons to begin recording. While recording, you can:

-Tap the white Shutter button to snap a still picture.

-Zoom the screen in or out by pinching it. Tap the Record button or Tap either volume catch to stop recording.

Record a Slow-motion Video

Recording a video in Slo-mo mode makes your video records in the normal way, but you see the slow-motion impact when you play it back. Also, you can edit your video to ensure that the slow-motion effect starts and stops at a time you set.

Capture a Time-lapse Video Mode

Record videos at selected periods to create a Time-lapse video of events happening during that period. Select the time-lapse mode, then place your iPhone where you intend to capture a scene in motion. Tap the recording button to start recording.

Edit Pictures and Videos with Content Outside the Frame

When "Capture Outside the Frame" is enabled in Settings, content situated outside the intended area shows up when you utilize the crop, fix, and viewpoint tools to add effects in the Photos application. To capture this content when you snap pictures, go to Settings, tap Camera, then enable Photos Capture Outside the Frame.

At the point when you record "QuickTake" videos, Camera, by itself, capture content outside the frame. Also, you can disable Videos Capture Outside the Frame in Settings. However, if these contents are not put into use to make edits, it will be deleted after 30 days.

Preserve Camera Settings

You can preserve your recent camera mode, filter, lighting, Live Photo settings, as well as other effects you used so they're not reset when next you open Camera.

Go to Settings, tap Camera, then tap Preserve Settings. You can choose to enable:

Camera Mode: this maintains the last camera mode you utilized, for example, Video or Pano.

Creative Controls: maintains the recent filter, lighting effect, and other settings you utilized.

Live Photo: maintains the Live Photo setting.

Adjust HDR Camera Settings on iPhone

HDR (High Dynamic Range) in Camera provides you with great shots in high-contrast circumstances. iPhone takes multiple pictures in quick progression at various exposures and mixes them to display more highlights and shadow detail to your pictures.

The iPhone utilizes HDR (for the back camera and the front camera) when it works best. For best outcomes, keep the iPhone stable and prevent subject motion. Any adjustments you intend to make to the HDR component can be done in the camera section in Settings.

Scan a QR Code with the iPhone Camera

You can utilize the Camera to check Quick Response (QR) codes for connections to sites, applications, coupons, tickets, and so much more. The camera consequently identifies and highlights a QR code.

To read a QR code, open the camera app and position the iPhone so that the code is captured, and it appears on the screen.

Chapter Twenty-Five

Utilizing the Phone Clock

Utilize the Clock application to check the local time in various time regions around the world.

Tap World Clock, Tap Edit to go through your list of cities, then you can:

-**Include a city**: Tap the Add button, then pick a city.

-**Delete a city:** Tap the Delete button.

-**Rearrange the cities:** Drag the Reorder button up or down.

Set an Alert or Sleep Time Plan on iPhone

In the Clock application, you can put in place an alarm that plays a sound or vibration at a particular time. Also, you can set a sleep time plan that prompts you when it's time rest or sleep and plays a sound or vibration when it's time to wake up based on your settings.

Set an Alert

Tap Alarm, then tap the Add button. Set the time, then go further to select certain options such as Repeat (to select the days of the week), Sound or tone of the alarm, Snooze (give yourself additional minutes), and label (to give a tag or name to the alarm), tap Save. To change or delete the alarm, tap Edit.

Set a Bedtime Plan

Tap Bedtime at the base of the screen, tap Set Up, then adhere to the on-screen directions. Or just simply enable Bedtime Schedule.

Change your Bedtime Plan

To do this, you can:

Select the days of the week for the alarm to be active.

Change your sleep and wake times by moving the bedtime button and the Wake button.

Disable sleep time reminders by tapping the Back button. Tap Options, then Tap Bedtime Reminder, then tap None. In Options, you can as well enable or disable Do Not Disturb during Bedtime, track your time in bed, and set your wake-up sound and volume

Use the Clock or Stopwatch on iPhone

In the Clock application, you can count down from a predetermined time using the timer. You can as well utilize the stopwatch to gauge the span of an event.

Set the Clock

Tap the timer, then set the length of time and a sound to play when the timer ends. A useful situation to implement this is when it seems you'll fall asleep while playing a song or video, you can set the clock to stop the playback. Tap "When Timer Ends," then Tap "Stop Playing at the base." Tap Start.

The clock proceeds regardless of whether you open another application or if the iPhone goes to sleep.

Track Time with the Stopwatch

Tap Stopwatch in the clock application. To switch between the digital and analog displays, swipe the stopwatch. Tap Start, the timing proceeds regardless of whether you open another application or if the iPhone goes to sleep. Tap Lap to record a lap or split. Tap Stop to record terminal time. Tap Reset to void the stopwatch.

Compass

Use the compass on iPhone

The Compass application provides you with information about where the iPhone is pointing, your present area, and elevation.

See your Bearings, Directions, and Elevations

Your coordinates, bearings, and elevation are displayed at the base of the screen. For precise bearings, hold the iPhone in a supine manner to adjust the line of sight at the center of the compass. Tap the compass dial to lock in your present direction.

A red band will be displayed when you're deviating from that path. To view your location in Maps, tap the coordinates at the base of the screen.

Permit Compass to Access your Location

If Compass doesn't have access to your location, ensure you've enabled Location Services. Go to Settings, select Privacy, tap Location Services, then turn on Location Services. Proceed to tap Compass, then Tap "While Using the App."

Chapter Twenty-Six

Facetime on iPhone

Set up FaceTime

In the FaceTime application, you can engage in video or audio calls with people if they have an iPhone, iPad, or any iOS device. You can capture a particular period during your conversation by taking a FaceTime Live Photo. Go to Settings, select FaceTime, then turn on FaceTime.

If you intend to have the option of taking Live Photos during FaceTime calls enabled, turn on FaceTime Live Photos. Then, input the telephone number, Apple ID, or email address you intend to use with FaceTime

Make and Receive FaceTime Calls on the iPhone

Provided your phone has an active Internet connection and with your Apple ID, you can make and receive calls on the FaceTime application.

Make a FaceTime Call

In FaceTime, tap the Add button at the upper right segment of the screen. Input the name or number you intend to call in the entry field at the top, then Tap Video to make a video call or Tap Audio to make a FaceTime audio call.

You can as well tap the "Add Contact" button to open Contacts and begin your call from that point or tap a contact in your rundown of FaceTime calls to rapidly make a call.

Begin FaceTime Call from Message Conversation

While you're in a message conversation, you can start a video call with that contact. Tap the profile picture or name of the contact at the top of the conversation, then Tap FaceTime. Begin a group FaceTime call.

In the FaceTime application, about 32 people can participate in a Group FaceTime call. To initiate a Group FaceTime call, tap the Add button at the upper right part of the screen, then input the names or numbers of the individuals you intend to bring in into the entry field at the top.

You can even tap the Add Contact button to open Contacts and include individuals from there.

Select Video to make a video call or Audio to make an audio call.

Every member shows up in a tile on the screen. At the point when a member talks or you tap the tile, that tile moves to the front and turns out to be more prominent. Tiles that can't fit on the screen show up in a row at the base. To reach a member you don't see, swipe through the row.

Join a Group FaceTime Call

When you're invited to join a Group FaceTime call, you see the incoming call. In case you decline the call, you get a notification that you can tap to join the call whenever it is active.

Leave a Group FaceTime Call

To leave a group call, tap the Leave call button. However, the call stays active if at least two members remain.

Take a Live Photo in FaceTime on iPhone

When you're on a video call the FaceTime application, you can take a FaceTime Live Photo to capture a particular period of your discussion. The camera records what happens just before and after you snap the picture, including the sound/audio, so you can see and hear it later simply how it occurred.

To take a FaceTime Live Photo, first ensure FaceTime Live Photos is turned on in Settings > FaceTime, after that, do any of these:

-If you're on a call with another individual, Tap the shutter button.

-If you're on a Group FaceTime call, tap the tile of the individual you intend to photograph, then Tap the Full-Screen button, then tap the shutter button.

You will be notified about when the picture was taken, and when the Live Photo is saved in your Photos app.

Become an Animoji or Memoji

During a FaceTime call, tap the Effects button. If the Effects button is not displayed, tap the screen. Tap the Animoji button, then select an Animoji or Memoji. The other caller will hear what you state, however, it is your Animoji or Memoji they'll see doing the talking.

Furthermore, you can add camera effects to your FaceTime calls, use filters to change your appearance, add labels, and even stickers when you tap on the Add Effects button.

Leave a FaceTime Call

Tap the screen and Tap the Leave call button.

-Change to a Messages discussion

To change your discussion to Messages, tap the screen, swipe up over the controls, then tap the Messages button.

Block Undesirable Callers in FaceTime

In the FaceTime application, voice calls, FaceTime calls, and instant messages from undesirable contacts can be blocked. Go to Settings, select FaceTime, Tap Blocked Contacts. Move down, then tap "Add New" at the base of the list. Select a contact that you intend to block.

Chapter Twenty-Seven

Handling Files on the iPhone

Connecting Devices or Servers on iPhone

You can utilize the Files application to obtain access to records stored on external gadgets or servers, for example, USB drives and SD cards, document servers, and other cloud storage providers like Box and Dropbox, after you connect them to your iPhone.

When you connect a USB drive to your iPhone or insert an SD card into your iPhone, tap Browse at the base of the screen to view the content of these external storage media. Then Tap the name of the gadget beneath Locations. In case you don't see Locations, tap Browse again at the base of the screen.

To disengage the gadget, remove it from the connector on the iPhone.

Connect to a PC or file server

Tap the More button at the crest of the Browse screen. In case the More button isn't displayed, tap Browse. Then, tap "Connect to Server." Input a nearby hostname or a system address, then tap Connect. You can connect as a guest or as a registered User.

Tap Next, go further to select the server volume or folder being shared in the Browse screen. To disengage from the server, tap the Eject button close to the server in the Browse screen.

Add a Cloud Storage Service

Download the application from the App Store, open the application, and adhere to the on-screen directions. Open Files, then Tap "Browse" at the base of the screen. Tap More Locations (underneath Locations), then enable the service.

To go through the content, tap Browse at the base of the screen, then select the name of the storage below Locations.

Browse and Open Documents and Folders

Tap Browse at the base of the screen, then select an item on the Browse screen.

To open a document or folder, tap the item. However, if you haven't installed the application that made the document, a quick display of the file opens in Quick Look.

Change to List Display or Icon Display

From an open area or folder, haul down from the center of the screen, then tap the List View button select the required option.

Change how Documents and Folders are Arranged

From an open folder, drag down from the center of the screen. Tap "Sorted by," then pick an option: Name, Date, Size, Types, or Tags.

Create a Folder

Open an area or a current organizer. Drag down the page of the screen, then Tap the More button, and select New Folder. If New Folder isn't displayed, that implies that you can't make a folder in that area.

Rename or Make Changes to File or Folder

Touch and hold the document or folder, then select an option. To modify several files simultaneously, tap Select and make your selections than pick an option at the bottom of the screen.

Send Records from Files on iPhone

You can send a duplicate of any document in the Files application to other people. On the off chance that you have a file, you need to send that isn't digitized, you can scan it with Files first.

Send a File

Touch and hold the record, then Tap Share. To send a miniaturized rendition of the file, tap ComTap before you tap Share. Then, hold the compacted rendition of the document (identified as a zip file), and tap Share. Then select the means through which you want to send the file (for instance, AirDrop, Messages, or Mail), then tap Send.

Scan a File

Tap the More button at the crest point of the Browse screen, then Tap "Scan Documents."

Change Access and Consent Settings for Everybody

In case you're the owner of a shared document or folder, you can change its access whenever you want to. However, the people you share the link with are also affected.

Touch and hold the item, then tap the Share button, Tap Show People, then tap Share Options. Change either or both of the alternatives.

-Access choice: When you change the access option from "Anybody with the link" to "Just individuals you invite," the first link no longer becomes active for anybody, and just individuals with whom you've sent a new invitation from you can open the document or folder.

-Permission option: When you change the authorization option, every individual who has the document open when you change the permission is notified. New settings become active when the alert is removed.

Chapter Twenty-Eight

Using the Health App on iPhone

Obtain Health and Fitness Information on iPhone

You can include other information like body weight and sugar intake, and track extra information with different applications, (for example, nutrition and fitness applications) and gadgets that are with Health, (for example, Apple Watch, AirPods, scales).

Manually Update your Health Profile

At your first time of opening the Health app, you're required to create a health profile with fundamental data, for example, your date of birth and sex. In case you don't fill in all the required data, you can update your profile later. Tap your profile picture at the edge of the Summary screen, if your profile picture isn't displayed, tap Summary at the base of the screen.

Tap Health Profile, then Tap Edit.

Collect information from different sources

From Apple Watch

After you pair iPhone with Apple Watch, an intermittent heart rate measurement, details about the activities you partake in, and more are sent from Apple Watch to Health.

From Earphones

After you connect EarPods, AirPods, and other earphones that support Health, to your iPhone, the earphones' sound levels are naturally sent to Health.

-From an application that you have granted the permission to share your data to the Health app.

From Another Gadget

Adhere to the setup procedure for the gadget. In case it is a Bluetooth gadget, you have to pair it with the iPhone. Adhere to the guidelines that accompanied the gadget to set it in discovery mode, go to Settings > Bluetooth, turn on Bluetooth, then tap the name of the device.

Display your Highlights

Tap the Summary tab at the base of the screen, then move down to view these details about your ongoing health and fitness information. Tap the Details button to obtain access to additional details.

View Subcategories in the Health Categories

Tap Browse at the base to show the Health Categories screen, then you can select a category. Tap the search box and input the name of a category.

To check details about any of the information, tap the Details button. Depending on the information type, you will be given some of the following options to do:

-View data by weekly, monthly, or yearly schedule by Taping the tabs at the highest point of the screen.

-Manually input data: Tap Add Data at the top of the screen.

-Transfer a data type to Favorites on the Summary screen: Enable Add to Favorites. If this option isn't displayed, scroll down on the page.

-View which applications and gadgets are permitted to share information: Tap Data Sources and Access underneath Options.

-Delete information: Tap Show All Data beneath Options, swipe left on data entry, then tap Delete. To delete all information, tap Edit, then Tap Delete All.

-Change the unit of measurement: Tap Unit beneath Options, then select an alternate unit of measurement.

Begin Cycle Tracking

Tap Browse at the base of the screen, then Tap Cycle Tracking.

Tap Get Started, then adhere to the on-screen directions.

To help improve expectations for your period and fertility window, enter the required details about your last period

Log your Cycle Data

Log a period day: Tap a day in the timetable at the top of the screen. To log the period flow level for that day, tap Period beneath Cycle Log, then select an option. Or on the other hand tap "Add Period" at the top, then select days from the monthly calendar.

Logged days are indicated by solid red circles. To delete a logged day, tap it.

Log symptoms: Drag the displayed timeline at the crest of the screen to choose a day, tap Symptoms, then select the necessary options, and tap Done. Days with symptoms are indicated by purple dots.

-Log spotting: Drag the timeline to choose a day, tap Spotting, tap "Had Spotting," then tap Done.

Tap Options to include other categories

View the Cycle Course of Events

Tap Browse at the base of the screen, then taps Cycle Tracking. Timeline details are shown in this configuration:

Strong red circles: Days you logged for your period.

Purple dots: Days you logged for exhibiting symptoms.

Light red circles: Your period predictions. You can disable period predictions, just tap Option.

Light blue days: A forecast of your probable fertility window. However, this prediction should not be used as a method of birth control.

To choose other days, drag the timeline. Information that you logged for the selected days shows up under the Cycle Log.

Share Health and Fitness Information

You can grant permission to other applications to share health data with the Health application. For instance, if an Exercise application is installed on the iPhone, its exercise data can show up in the Health application. The exercise application can also peruse and utilize information, (for example, your pulse and weight) shared by different gadgets and apps.

Export and Share your Health Information

Tap your profile picture at the top of the Health screen. If a profile picture isn't displayed, tap Summary or Browse at the base of the screen, then scroll the page to the top.

Tap "Export all health data," then, select how you intend to the data.

Download Health Records

The Health application offers access to data from bolstered health organizations about your health conditions, medication, and more.

Set up Programmed Downloads

Tap your profile picture at the upper right, and Tap "Health Records." Then select any of these:

Set up your first download: Tap "Get Started."

Set up downloads for extra records: Tap "Add Account."

Input the name of an organization, for example, a health center or clinic, where you get your health records. Or then again, enter the name of the city or state where you live to go through a rundown of nearby health organizations.

Below "Available to Connect," Tap the Connect to Account button to move to the sign-in screen for your patient portal. Enter your username and password for the patient online portal of that organization, then adhere to the on-screen guidelines.

Delete Organization and its Records from Phone

Tap your profile picture on the health screen, then Tap Health Records. Tap the name of an organization, then tap "Remove Account."

Create or Alter Details of Medical ID

Tap your profile picture or initials on the health screen. In case you don't see your profile picture or your initials, tap Summary or Browse at the base of the screen, then scroll to the top of the screen.

Tap Medical ID, then do any of these:

Make a Medical ID: Tap Get Started.

Change your Medical ID: Tap Edit.

To automatically send your Medical ID data to emergency services when you call or message 911 or make use of Emergency SOS, turn on "Share During Emergency Call." To allow immediate responders and others to see your Medical ID when your iPhone is locked, "Show When Locked" is enabled by default. Try not to disable this choice except if you need to keep responders from checking your Medical ID.

Register as Organ Contributor

In the Health application, you can register to be an organ, eye, or tissue donor with Donate Life America. Your choice to give is visible to others in your Medical ID. In case you later change your decision of donating, you can cancel your registration.

Back up your Health Information

Provided you signed in with your Apple ID, details about your health in the Health application are stored in iCloud. Your data is encoded as it transits between iCloud and your gadget and even while it's stored in iCloud. Also, you can back up your Health information by encoding a computer backup.

Chapter Twenty-Nine

Concept of Notes

Compose Notes on iPhone

Utilize the Notes application to write down or compose detailed information with checklist, pictures, scanned documents, weblinks, manually written notes, and sketches.

Create and Design a New Note

If you'll like to use voice control, summon Siri and say something like: "Make a new note." Or follow the manual process. Tap the New Note button and enter your content. The starting line of the note turns into the note's title. To change the text style, Tap the Text Styles button denoted by Aa. Tap Done to save the note.

Include a Checklist

In a note, tap the Checklist button, here you can:

-Add things to the rundown: Enter the content, Tap Return to input the next item.

-Swipe left or right on an item to adjust the indentation on the item.

-Mark an item as complete: Tap the vacant circle close to the item to include a checkmark.

-Rearrange items: Touch and hold the vacant circle or checkbox close to the item, then drag the item to another spot on the list.

-Oversee items in the rundown: Tap the list to see the menu, Tap the "Show More Items" button, tap Checklist, then select an option.

To arrange checked items in your note automatically, go to Settings > Notes > Sort Checked Items, then select "Automatically."

Draw in Notes on iPhone

You can create drawings or make a handwritten note with your finger in the note's application. This is done when you make use of the markup devices, colors and draw straight lines with the ruler.

Add a Photograph or Video

Tap the displayed Camera button in Notes to snap a photograph or record a video or tap Photo Library to include media items that are already on your phone. To adjust the display size of an attachment, touch and hold the attachment, then select either Small Images or Large Images.

Scanning and Converting Document into Note

Tap the Camera button in the note's application, tent Tap Scan Documents. Position the iPhone on the document properly to ensure that the page shows up on the screen, the iPhone, by itself, captures the page, tap Save. To make changes to the saved document, tap the document and do any of these:

- Include more pages by Taping the Add Scan button.
- Crop the picture by Taping the Crop button.
- Tap the Show Filters button to add a filter to the scanned image.
- Tap the Rotate button to change the orientation of the image.
- Tap the Share button, then tap markup tools include annotations or signatures.
- Tap the Delete Scan button to delete the scanned version of the document.

Create, Rename, Move, or Delete a Folder

- Tap to select New Folder in the folders list, then type in a name for your folder, this creates the folder. If you want to set up a subfolder, hold a folder and drag it into another folder
- Move a folder to another position: Swipe left on the folder, Tap the Move Folder button, then select another location to move the folder to

- Swipe left on a folder, then tap the trash icon. This deletes the folder; you can recover deleted notes in the Recently Deleted folder
- Search inside a note for typed and handwritten content
- Open the note you intend to search for. Tap the Share button, then tap Find in Note. Type the content you're searching for in the search box.

Share Notes and Collaborate on iPhone

In the Notes application, you can send a duplicate of note to other people. Also, you can invite individuals to collaborate on a note or an item of notes in iCloud, and changes made to these items will be made visible to everyone.

Collaborate on Note

Collaborators will be able to view changes made by everyone. However, they must all be signed in to iCloud to edit the note. Open the note you need to share. Locked notes can't be collaborated on. Tap the Add People button, tap Share Options, then pick either "Can make changes" or "View only."

Decide How to Send Invitation

To include or expel collaborators or quit collaborating, tap the View Participants button.

Create Password for Notes

Go to Settings > Notes > Password.

Input a password and add a hint to assist you with recollecting the password. For additional security, you can enable Touch ID. With the Touch ID, you can have access to your notes, however, you won't be able to view your locked notes, and Apple can't assist you with restoring access to those locked notes.

Furthermore, you can reset your notes password in settings, however, this doesn't give you access to locked notes. The recent password is only effective for notes you lock from that moment.

Lock a Note

Notes can only be locked on your gadget and in iCloud. However, you can't lock note of that have PDFs, sound, video, Keynote, Pages, note that are synchronized with a different account.

Swipe left on the note in the notes list, then Tap the lock. Alternatively, you can open the note, Tap the Share button, then tap Lock Note. To unlock a note, tap the Share button, then Tap Remove Lock.

Chapter Thirty

Voice Memos

Make a Recording in Voice Memos.

The voice memo app is placed in the utility folder on the iPhone, with this app, you can employ the iPhone as a versatile portable gadget to record individual notes, study classes, music thoughts, and many more. You can even manipulate your recorded items with editing tools like, replace, and resume.

When you enable Voice Memos in iCloud settings, your recordings show up and update automatically on every device where you've signed the same Apple ID.

Make a Recording

Tap the Record button to start recording. You can then modify the recording level, by adjusting the distance of the microphone from what you're recording. Tap the Stop button to end the recording session.

If Location Services has been enabled in Settings, your recordings will be saved with the name of your location, otherwise, it will be saved as "New Recording." To change the name, tap the recording, then Tap the name and input another name.

While recording on the voice memo app, you can make use or another application. As long as the audio or video is not played on the app, it doesn't interfere with the recording. Tap the home button to take you to the home screen on your iPhone, then open the app. However, voice memo also records other sounds it picks up from you and even the sounds on your device while using another app.

To revert to the voice memo app, Tap the little red icon at the crest of the screen.

Play an account in Voice Memos on iPhone

Tap a recorded item in the voice memo application and use the onscreen controls to control your playback while listening.

Control	Description
▶	Play
❚❚	Pause
⏪15	Skip backward 15 seconds
15⏩	Skip forward 15 seconds

Edit or Delete an Account in Voice Memos

The voice memo application comes with some editing tools that you require to manipulate your recordings. These editing tools include ones you can use to expel parts you don't need, record over parts, or replace a whole recording.

Trim a Recording

Open the recorded item in the voice memo application, and Tap the More button, then tap Edit Recording. Tap the Trim button at the top of the screen, then adjust the yellow trim handles to encase the area you intend to keep or delete. You can zoom in screen to ensure accurate trimming.

To listen to the part of the recording you've encased, tap the Play button. To retain the selection, which implies deleting the other parts of the recording, tap Trim, or to delete the selection, Tap Delete. Tap Save and Tap Done.

Delete an Account

You either open the recording in the voice memo application or Tap the Delete button. Or, Tap Edit at the top Voice memo list, select the recordings, then delete them. Deleted recordings move to the "Recently Deleted" folder in the Voice Memos list, where they're retained for 30 days before they finally get deleted. You can change the extent to which deleted recordings are retained in the Voice memo section in Settings. To permanently delete a recording in the Recently Deleted folder, tap the recording, then delete it.

To restore a deleted recording from the Recently Deleted folder, tap the recording and Tap Recover.

Duplicate a Recording

Duplicates of a recording can be made in the voice memo application which is helpful when you need another version of the recording. You can make changes to the duplicate, and even save it with another name.

Open a recording, and tap the More button, then select Duplicate.

The duplicate will be displayed directly below the original form of the recording in the list and has "copy" added to its name. You can tap the name, then input a new one.

Chapter Thirty-One

Apple Tv

Set up the Apple TV Application

The Apple TV application provides you with access to TV shows, movies, sports, and live news.

Subscribe to Apple TV+

Subscribing to Apple TV+ enables you to watch new, selective Apple Originals without ads. Stream Apple TV+ on iPhone, other Apple devices, supported TVs, or download Apple Originals to watch on offline mode on iPhone. With Family Sharing, up to six relatives can share the membership with no extra charge.

Tap Watch Now, scroll to the Apple TV+ line, then select any of these:

Begin a free Apple TV+ subscription for one year: Tap Enjoy one Year Free.

Begin a free 7-day trial: Tap Try Apple TV+

Begin a monthly subscription plan: Tap Subscribe.

Survey the subscription subtleties, then affirm with Touch ID or your Apple ID.

These options also apply to the Apple TV subscription.

Add Cable or Satellite Services

Go to Settings, tap TV Provider. Select your TV provider, then sign in with your provider details. In case your TV provider isn't displayed, sign indirectly from the application you intend to use.

Manage Linked Applications and Subscriptions

Tap the "My Account" button or your profile picture at the top screen. Then select any of these options:

Connected Apps: this enables or disables the application.

Manage Subscriptions: Tap a subscription plan to change or cancel it.

Clear Play History: delete your viewing history from all your Apple devices.

Discover Shows and Films

When you tap Watch Now in the TV application, several options of discovering movies and shows are displayed. You can browse by category, either movie, shows, sports, kids. You can also browse Apple TV+ or Apple TV channels for items. Furthermore, getting recommendations of items that are personalized for you, watching live news, and using the Up Next component are other ways of discovering movies.

Manage Shows and Movies on TV app

Tap an item to view its subtleties.

Watch Apple TV+ or Apple TV channels: If you've subscribed to that plan, tap Play. In case you're not a present subscriber, select Try It Free or Subscribe.

Tap "Open in" to view the recommended video application. Select another video application: If the title is obtained from different providers, scroll down to How to Watch, then select a provider.

Purchase or rent: Confirm your selection, then finish up with the payment.

After renting a movie, you have 30 days to begin watching it. After you begin viewing the film, you can play it over and over again as many times as you need for 48 hours, after which the rental time frame closes. At the point when the rental period ends, the film is deleted.

Download: Tap the Download button to download to your Library, which means you can then watch even when your iPhone isn't connected to the Internet.

Pre-order: Go through the details, then Tap Pre-Order. When the pre-requested item becomes available, your payment method is charged, and an email notification will be sent to you. If automatic download has been enabled on the iPhone, the item, by itself, starts to download to your iPhone.

Control playback in the Apple TV application

During playback, tap the screen to display the controls.

Remove a download

Tap Library, then Tap Downloaded. Swipe left on the item you intend to remove, and tap Delete. Deleting an item from your iPhone doesn't delete it from your purchases in iCloud. You can download the item to your iPhone again if need be.

▶	Play
❚❚	Pause
↺15	Skip backward 15 seconds; touch and hold to rewind
15↻	Skip forward 15 seconds; touch and hold to fast-forward
▭	Change the aspect ratio; if you don't see the scaling control, the video already fits the screen perfectly
🗩	Display subtitles and closed captions (if available)
⬓	Stream the video to other devices
✕	Stop playback

Chapter Thirty-Two

Apple Apps Store

Get applications, games, and text styles in the App Store on iPhone

The App Store application on the iPhone is where you can find new applications and games, download custom text styles, and learn certain tips as well. You can as well subscribe to Apple Arcade.

Find Applications, Games, and Fonts

For a quick result, you can summon Siri and say something like: "Search the App Store for football applications." Also, you can tap any of the tabs at the base of the App store screen depending on what you want.

Buy and Download an Application

To purchase an application, tap the price tag displayed below it. If the application is free (that is, it has no price tag), tap Get.

If the Download button is what is displayed rather than a price, that implies that you have already purchased the application, and you can download it again without paying any amount. Whenever required, confirm your Apple ID with Touch ID, or your password to complete your purchase.

While downloading, the icon of the app is displayed at the top of the Home screen with a progress indicator. When you download an app containing fonts on your iPhone, open the app to install the fonts. You can change fonts in Settings

Gift or Redeem an App Store and iTunes Gift Voucher

Tap My Account button or your profile picture at the top of the screen. Select any of these options:

-Redeem Gift Card or Code

-Send Gift Card by Email

Manage your App Store Purchases, Subscriptions, and Settings on iPhone

You can manage your subscription activities, review, rate, and download purchases made by you or other members of your family. Furthermore, you can modify your preferences for the App Store in Settings.

Change your App Store Settings

Go to Settings, tap [your name], select iTunes and App Store, then select any of these options:

- Automatically download applications bought on your other Apple gadgets: Below Automatic Downloads, tap "Apps" to enable it.
- Automatically update applications by turning on App Updates.
- Manage of cellular data usage for application downloads: To permit downloads to use cellular data, turn on

Automatic Downloads. To set whether you need to be requested consent for downloads more than 200 MB or all applications, Tap App Downloads.

- Turn on Video Auto play to automatically play apps preview videos.

Chapter Thirty-Three

Apple iBooks

Find and Purchase Books in Apple iBooks

The iBooks application on the iPhone lets you discover, search for and buy books from Apple Books, and afterward peruse or listen to them (in case of audiobooks) in the application.

Open Books, then Tap Book Store or Audiobooks to check for titles or tap Search to search for a particular title. Tap a book cover to see more subtleties about the book, view a sample, listen to a review, or imprint as "Want to Read."

Tap Buy to purchase a title, or Tap Get to download a free title.

Read Books in the iBooks Application on iPhone

You can make use of the "Reading Now" and "Library tabs" at the base of the screen in the books application to view the books you're perusing, the books you intend to read, your collection of books, and other options.

Reading Now: This tab gives you access to the books and audiobooks that you're reading or listening to at that moment. Scroll down to view items you've just recently included to your "Want to Read" collection and books you've gone through.

Also, you can set and monitor every day and yearly reading objectives.

Library: The library tab displays the entire items (books, audiobooks, series, and PDFs) you got from the Book Store or manually added to your library. Furthermore, you can tap Collections to see your books arranged into collections, for example, Want to Read, My Samples, Audiobooks, and Finished.

Read a Book

Tap the Reading Now or Library tab, then Tap the book cover to open a book. You can swipe to change book pages and navigate through the page.

Tap either right or left side of the book to move to the next or previous page respectively. You can also swipe left or right to do this.

Go to a particular page: Tap the page and move the slider at the base of the screen left or right. Or then again, tap the Search button and enter a page number, and tap the page number in the search box.

Close a book: Tap the center of the page to display the controls and tap the Back button. Text styles and display appearances can also be modified while you are on a page. Tap the Appearance button denoted by aA, then select the displayed options to make the adjustments.

Bookmark a Page

When you close a book, the present page you are in the book is automatically saved, therefore you don't have to include a bookmark. Bookmark pages you intend to come back to another time.

Tap the Bookmark Ribbon to include a bookmark; tap it again to cancel the bookmark. To view every one of your bookmarks, tap the Table of Contents button (denoted by three horizontal bars), then tap Bookmarks.

Highlight or Underline Content in a Book

Touch and hold a text, then move your fingers across the screen and grab sections to enlarge the selection. Tap Highlight and tap the Highlight Color Chooser button to select a highlight color or to underline.

To delete a highlight or underline, tap the content, then tap the Trash button. To view the entirety of your highlighted text, tap the Table of Contents button, then Tap Notes.

Add a Note

Touch and hold a word, then carefully move your fingers across to grab point to modify the selection. Tap Note, then use the keyboard to enter the content of the note, tap Done. Swipe left on a note to delete it.

Play a Book Recording

Tap the Reading Now tab or the Audiobooks collection in your Library, then tap the audiobook cover, then select any of these options:

-Touch and hold the rounded-arrow buttons or slide and hold the book cover to skip. You can modify the number of seconds that skipping advances in the Books section in Settings.

- Tap the playback speed in the lower-left edge to select playback speed. 1x is the typical playback speed.

- Tap the Sleep button to set a sleep timer, then select the duration.

- Move to a particular time: Drag the playhead underneath the audiobook cover.

- Create a collection and add books to it

You can set up your collections of books to customize your library.

Tap Library, Tap Collections, and tap New Collection. Give the collection a name, then tap Done.

To add a book to the collection, tap the More Info button beneath the book cover (or on the book's subtleties page in the Book Store), tap Add to Collection, then choose the collection.

You can add a particular book to numerous collections.

Sort Books in your Library

Sorting books changes how they are categorized and displayed. Scroll down in the library and Tap Sort or Sort by. You can then sort books based on the author, title, or sort manually.

Remove Books, Recordings and PDFs

You can delete books, audiobooks, and PDFs from Reading Now and your library collections, or conceal them on your iPhone.

Tap Library, then Tap Edit. Select the items you intend to remove, then tap the Trash button and pick an option.

To unhide books that you have concealed, tap Reading Now, tap your account icon, then tap Manage Hidden Purchases.

Open PDFs in Books

Hold the PDF attachment, then Tap Copy to Books. Alternatively, you can tap the PDF attachment to open it, Tap the Share button, then Tap Copy to Books.

Chapter Thirty-Four

iTunes Store

Get Music, TV Shows, and Movies from the iTunes Store

Select any of these options in the iTunes store:

Music, movies, or TV shows: browse the items based on their categories, to make your browsing more exclusive, Tap Genres at the top of the screen.

Charts: To get to know what's popular on iTunes

-**Search:** Input what you intend to search for, then Tap search on the keyboard.

More: Go through superb recommendations and tones.

Tap an item to view additional details about it. You can watch the trailer of a movie, preview a song, or Tap the share button to share an item, gift the item or even add the item to your Wishlist.

Redeem or Give an App Store or iTunes Gift Card

Tap Music scroll to the bottom of the page, then Tap Redeem or Send Gift.

Manage your iTunes Store Purchases and Settings

You can evaluate and download music, movies, and other items purchased by you or other family members in the iTunes store application. Furthermore, you can customize your inclinations for the iTunes store in Settings.

Change your iTunes Store Settings

Go to Settings, tap [your name], select iTunes, and App store. Then, select any of these options: -Beneath automatic downloads, turn on Music to automatically download music purchased on your other Apple gadgets.

-Beneath cellular data, disable Automatic Downloads to restrict iTunes store downloads to Wi-Fi connections.

Podcasts

Find Podcasts on iPhone

Use the podcast application to discover and play free shows, more like the radio of TV shows, but are more inclined to a particular field such as science, comedy, politics, news, agriculture, and more. When you subscribe to a particular show on the podcast app, new episodes of the shows are automatically downloaded when they're released.

Discover and Subscribe to Shows

Tap Browse to View featured shows and top charts. You can as we browse items based on the categories they belong to or their providers. Furthermore, you can search for an item on a podcast based on the title, topic, or area.

To subscribe to a show, tap the show to display its information page, then Tap Subscribe.

Listen to Subscribed Shows

Tap Listen Now, to download an episode of a show for offline listening, Tap the download button displayed near the episode. If the download button isn't displayed, that implies that the has already been downloaded.

To receive notifications whenever an episode is released, Tap the Notification Settings button.

Play a Podcast

Tap an episode of a show. Then, Tap the player at the base of the screen to open the Now Playing Screen, this provides you with more playback controls. Swipe up on the now playing screen to display other options such as the sleep timer, episode notes, and more.

▶ Play

Ⅱ Pause

(15) Jump back 15 seconds

(30) Jump forward 30 seconds

1× Choose a faster or slower playback speed

(((▲))) Stream the audio to other devices

••• Choose more actions such as sharing the episode or adding it to your queue.

Manage your Subscriptions

Tap the Library tab, then select a show to display its information page, then Tap the more info button, which provides you with the following options:

-Tap Settings to alter the sequence of episodes playback, manage downloads, disable notifications, and more.

-Unsubscribe from a show to downloading recent episodes.

-Tap Delete from Library to remove all the episodes.

Tap delete when you swipe left on an episode to remove the episode.

For Podcasts shows you haven't subscribed to, Tap the add podcast button next to an episode to include the episode in your library.

In the Podcasts section in Settings, you can modify your preferences such as enabling Podcasts synchronization to ensure that your subscriptions are updated on all your devices where you've signed in with the same Apple ID, restricting downloads from using cellular data and more.

Chapter Thirty-Five

Apple Pay

Keep Cards and Wallet on iPhone

For quick access, the Wallet application stores your cards and passes in a similar place on the iPhone.

Apple Pay Cards include Apple Card, Apple Cash, credit, charge, store, travel, and prepaid cards. Passes, on the other hand, entail movie and occasion tickets, coupons, reward cards, student Identity cards, among others.

Add a Credit or Debit Card

In Wallet, Tap the Add button, you might be required to sign in with your Apple ID. Then select any of these options:

Include a new card: Place your iPhone on the card to capture the details of the card or type in the details by yourself.

Include your previous cards: Select the card linked with your Apple ID, cards you use with Apple Pay on your different gadgets, or cards that you expelled. Tap Continue, then input the CVV number of each card.

Use a Rewards Card

At certain stores, you can obtain or redeem rewards when you use Apple Pay. Add your rewards card to your Wallet. At the payment spot in the store, present your rewards card by holding the iPhone close to the contactless reader.

To enable your rewards card to show up automatically when you're in the store, Tap the More button on the card, then enable Automatic Selection.

Set up and Use Apple Cash on iPhone

When an amount of cash is sent to in Messages, it's joined to your Apple Cash card in the Wallet application. You can make use of Apple Cash instead of any situation where you would Apple Pay. Furthermore, you can transfer the amount in your Apple Cash to your bank account.

Set up Apple Cash

Go to Settings, Tap Wallet, and Apple Pay, then enable Apple Cash. Alternatively, in Messages, you can just send or receive a payment – View the data for a card and change its settings. In Wallet, tap the card, then Tap the More button. Tap Transactions to display your recent history. To conceal this data, disable Transaction History. To view all your activities on Apple, Pay, check the statement from your card provider.

Show the last four digits of the card number and Device Account Number, which is the Number transmitted to the merchant. You can also Modify the charging address, and even remove a card from your wallet.

Remove Cards from Apple Pay

In case your iPhone gets lost or stolen, you can make use of the Find My iPhone component to help find and secure your iPhone. You can remove your associated cards on the misplaced iPhone by using another gadget. To do that, you can use any of the following options:

On a Mac or PC: Sign in to your Apple ID account. In the Devices section, click the misplaced iPhone. Beneath the list of cards, Tap Remove all.

On another iPhone, iPad, or iPod contact: Go to Settings, tap [your name], select the misplaced device, then Tap Remove All Cards.

-Call the card providers to help you with it.

A removed card can be added again when you input the details. However, if you sign out of iCloud, all your bank cards for Apple Pay are expelled from the iPhone. You can include the cards again whenever you sign in with your Apple ID.

Add Pass

You might be required to include a pass in an application after you carry out an activity, for example, buying a ticket. Alternatively, you can tap Add to Apple Wallet when you come across it in your mail or messages, Web browser, wallet-enabled apps, AirDrop sharing, QR code, or bar code.

To scan the code, open the Camera application, then position the iPhone so that the code shows up on the screen.

The iPhone SE 2020 is a perfect choice if you want a new pint-sized iPhone, with superb specs, that's easy and simple to use and still supports all the best apps, reliable for several years, and gives you the best outcome with prices from just $399, which is a budget-friendly price when compared to other iPhones with similar specifications. Overall, the iPhone SE 2020 is a good deal.

www.ingramcontent.com/pod-product-compliance
Lightning Source LLC
LaVergne TN
LVHW041203050326
832903LV00020B/439